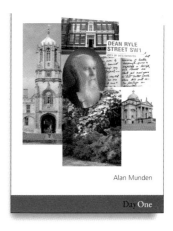

Alan Munden

Day One

Series Editor: Brian H Edwards

Day One

TRAVEL
WITH

Bishop J C **Ryle**
Prince of tract writers

52

❷ 'My little parish of three hundred parishioners'

J C Ryle's small Suffolk parish was dominated by the all-powerful John Tollemache. Ryle was twice married at Helmingham, and after Matilda and Jessie died he became a single parent responsible for five young children. While he was the squire of Helmingham Ryle wrote about eighty of his tracts

In February 1844 Ryle became the rector of St Mary, Helmingham, nine miles north of Ipswich, where he remained until 1861. The area was an isolated rural community and the main crops were wheat, barley and beans. There is no village as such, and the parish consists mostly of the Helmingham estate. In 1841 there were forty-eight houses and a population of 284; twenty years later there were 1041 two houses and a population of 520. Apart from John Tollemache and the rector there were no professional people living in the locality—the rest were tenant farmers, agricultural labourers and domestic servants.

Helmingham Hall and the parish church

The vicarage was adjacent to the estate's deer park around Helmingham Hall. When Ryle arrived, the rectory needed to be improved, and he stayed at the Hall while the work took place. The Tollemache family frequently entertained the great and the good and often eighteen excise or people sat down for an evening meal. Each morning

and evening Ryle led prayers for the household and Sunday was strictly observed at the Hall. Given Ryle's own social background he would have been quite at home with the Tollemache family and their numerous visitors, and the contacts he made were to become invaluable to him.

Since the Norman Conquest generations of the Tollemache family have lived in Suffolk, and they moved to Helmingham in the late 13th century. In 1822 John Tollemache inherited the Hall from his aunt and carried out an extensive restoration programme. From 1841 he was the MP for South Cheshire, then from 1868 for West Cheshire, and in 1876 he was created Baron Tollemache of Helmingham. Though politically he was a liberal conservative, he was known as 'the labourer's Lord'. Yet Ryle observed that his parishioners 'were not interesting, living in fact in a state of servile subjection to Mr Tollemache.'

In August 1846 John Tollemache married his first

Facing page: A studio portrait of J C Ryle aged about forty

56

Above: The former Helmingham rectory once occupied by Ryle and his family is now a private house. A later rector described the house as being 'dark and gloomy' and with a very small garden

Above: The former Helmingham Sunday school

Above: Helmingham school was opened in April 1854

out and about throughout Suffolk, preaching in other churches and speaking at meetings in the town and villages. He spent some time in his study—reading and writing and adding to his large library. Over the years also became a substantial collector and after his death he left most of his books to the diocese of Liverpool. During his seventeen years at Helmingham, he composed about eighty tracts, most of which were reprinted in the first seven volumes of *Home Truths* and later more appeared as chapters in his books; he also gathered collections of hymns and wrote devotional commentaries on Matthew, Mark and Luke.

The Religious Census

On 30 March 1851, the year of the Great Exhibition, a national Religious Census was conducted in the churches and chapels throughout England and Wales. It showed that out of a population of nearly eighteen million, only some 7,261,234 people had actually attended a

place of worship and of these only 52% had attended the Church of England. Every clergyman or minister was expected to complete a questionnaire and on his Census return Ryle recorded that St Mary's church could accommodate 130 people of whom 100 people had to pay for their seats and the rest were free. On 30 March there was a morning congregation of 96 adults and 10 afternoon congregation of 141 adults, and a Sunday school of 47 children. Over the previous twelve months the average congregation had been 130 adults in the morning

57

Left: A studio portrait of J C Ryle aged about forty. 'We look upon him as one of the leaders of a great party in the Church' (Archdeacon William Emery)

and 200 adults in the afternoon, together with a Sunday school of 40 children. Ryle noted that 'many sit in benches in the aisles' and there was a larger congregation in the summer than in the winter. He recorded too that his income now totals up of £340 from tithes, £45 from glebe land, and £2 from fees for conducting weddings and funerals.

Ryle the preacher and pastor

What was Ryle like when he preached? Shortly before he left Helmingham a visitor recorded his impressions: 'Mr Ryle is no orator, a rhetorician, rather than a reasoner ... he is an able rhetorician, and has a wonderful power of illustration, with these he works his way most successfully.' He preached without notes, and like many of the longest sermons listed by the 'twenty churchgoer' who recorded in the Suffolk Pulpit that 'few, we believe, could hear such a sermon, so marked he unmistakeable earnestness of purpose so vigorously and so simply illustrated, without wishing

for it a more extensive audience.'

While Ryle was a dedicated man of God he was also somewhat aloof. He confessed that 'I want get the reputation, which I never lost, of being unsociable, distant, reserved and indisposed to encourage friendship, and not at home anywhere except in the pulpit or on the platform.' Yet he was not without an angelical friends. It was his conviction that clergy should be set apart from secular matters and he criticised those who spoke at agricultural meetings and wore 'prizes for fat pigs, enormous bullocks, and large crops of turnips.' He was not prepared to make 'morning calls of courtesy and dining out, as others do.' However this sort of behaviour did not endear him to other people, but it has to be said that his reserve was also because he was a single, slightly bachelor. His standard was high, and he looked for 'a woman who was a real Christian, who was a real lady, and who was not a fool.'

Ryle's first marriage

J C Ryle married three times and his first two wives died young. In October 1845 he married Matilda Charlotte Louisa Plumptre. He was twenty-eight and she was twenty-two. Matilda was the youngest of the three daughters of John Plumptre MP of Fredville, Nonington in East Kent.

CONTENTS

© Day One Publications 2012   First printed 2012

A CIP record is held at The British Library   ISBN 978-1-84625-327-0

Published by Day One Publications Ryelands Road, Leominster, HR6 8NZ

℡ 01568 613 740 FAX 01568 611 473 email: sales@dayone.co.uk www.dayone.co.uk   All rights reserved

All Bible references quoted in this book are taken from the Authorised Version (the King James Version) of 1611 which would have been the translation used by J C Ryle. The author wants the reader to hear the voice of Ryle and so the many quotations are taken from his own writings. In the interests of brevity they are not referenced, but the author can give any sources that are required if requested from the publishers

Design: studiohope limited, www.studiohope.co.uk   Printed in Spain under supervision of MRM Graphics Ltd.

Dedication: Dedicated to those whose Christian lives have been enriched by reading the works of Bishop J C Ryle

Meet John Charles Ryle

A century and more after his death, the writings of one of the most prominent evangelical bishops of the 19th century are still read by Christians of all denominations. His devotional commentaries *Expository Thoughts on the Gospels*, the practical books like *Knots Untied* or *Holiness*, and his historical biographies like *Five English Reformers* and *Christian Leaders of the 18th Century* are valued resources for those who want to deepen their faith. Ryle was not a dry, stuffy theologian who cannot be understood, but someone who wrote with great clarity and practical application—and who made difficult theological ideas easy to grasp. Ryle was always *biblical* (he took scripture seriously), *evangelical* (he wanted people to became committed Christians), *protestant* (he fully endorsed the theological issues of the 16th century Reformation), and he was a *Puritan* (he loved and honoured the 17th century Puritans). Ryle was also an *Anglican* who believed in the value of the established Church in the life of the nation. Over the past 150 years 'Bishop Ryle', or 'J C Ryle' as he is better known, has helped thousands of people to come to faith in Christ and to mature as Christian believers. Ryle was a Church of England clergyman who lived for thirty-six years in rural Suffolk. During that time he wrote some 200 popular tracts, published books, preached in numerous churches, and spoke at national conferences and public meetings. As the first Bishop of Liverpool he was responsible for creating new diocesan structures, the opening of numerous churches and mission rooms, and the ordination and appointment of additional clergy.

In this Travel Guide we take you in the steps of J C Ryle and throw some fresh light into his life, belief and personal convictions.

Facing page: John Charles Ryle the first Bishop of Liverpool, a photograph taken in 1888

1 A banker's son

J C Ryle's grandfather made his fortune from the silk industry; while his family were financially secure and enjoyed a privileged lifestyle they did not share his evangelical faith and the young Ryle grew up as a member of a nominal church-going family

The 'Royle' family originated from Lancashire before they moved to Cheshire, and from the 16th century they were known as 'Ryle'. Most of the family were farmers and the first documented ancestor, John Ryle, was the tenant of High Greaves Farm, in the township of Etchells in the parish of Northenden. Then it was rural, but is now an urban area west of Cheadle. High Greaves was sold in the mid-18th century and Thomas Ryle moved a few miles south and established himself in the growing industrial town of Macclesfield.

His son John Ryle (1744–1808) – JC Ryle's grandfather – became a prosperous landowner, banker and industrialist who made a large fortune from the silk trade. He was a committed evangelical Christian and actively supported John Wesley when the Methodist leader visited Macclesfield. Subsequently John Ryle gave the site for the Wesleyan Methodist chapel in Sunderland Street, and after the building became unsafe contributed £1,000 towards the new chapel.

Wesley and the Evangelicals
In March 1762 the evangelical revival began in Macclesfield through the ministry of John Oldham. In the following August, when Wesley preached in the town, he found forty believers each of whom had found peace with God.

Above: *John Ryle, the Christian industrialist and grandfather of J C Ryle*

Facing page: *The 108 Steps, Macclesfield by local artist Charles Frederick Tunnicliffe (1901–1979) who became well-known for his illustrations of birds and animals*

Left: Wesleyan Methodist chapel in Sunderland Street, erected in 1779 and enlarged in 1799

David Simpson (1745–1799)

David Simpson was one of the 300 to 500 Anglican clergy who became identified with the 18th century evangelical revival. After his conversion at Cambridge he became known as a Methodist and in his second curacy in Buckingham his powerful preaching made him unpopular. In 1772 he became the assistant curate at St Michael's chapel, Macclesfield, and again his preaching proved to be controversial. However he remained in post but there were tensions between himself and the senior curate. After Simpson failed to succeed him he became the minister of a private chapel erected by Charles Roe. John Wesley preached there on numerous occasions and stated, 'the new church here is far the most elegant that I have seen in the kingdom.'

After Christ Church was consecrated in 1779 Simpson became the first minister.

Above: David Simpson the minister of Christ Church, Macclesfield from 1779 to 1799

His preaching attracted large congregations and he continued to invite Wesley to preach. On Good Friday 1782, Wesley recorded, 'I preached for him morning and afternoon, and we administered the sacrament [of Holy Communion] to about 1,300 persons.' On a later visit Wesley remarked that 'the organ is one of the finest toned I ever heard, and the congregation singing with it make a sweet harmony.'

Simpson was diligent in his parish duties, opened a charity school and a Sunday school, published a hymn book and was a prolific author. Theologically he was an Arminian. He died twelve days before he planned to secede from the Church of England.

Above: *The interior of Christ Church, Macclesfield, which opened in 1775 and closed in 1981*

Above: *The Ryle family pew (originally no 37) on the south side of the nave in Christ Church*

Wesley frequently preached in Macclesfield, and in April 1776 reported that the congregation was too large for their usual place of meeting, so he 'preached on the [Park] Green, near Mr [John] Ryle's door. There are no mockers here and scarce an inattentive hearer. So mightily has the Word of God prevailed!'

Sadly, during most of his ministry Wesley had little public support from the evangelical clergy in the Church of England, but there were exceptions, like David Simpson of Macclesfield and William Grimshaw of Haworth (see in this series *William Grimshaw of Haworth* by Fred Perry).

The antagonism between Wesleyan Methodists and Anglican Evangelicals was because Wesley was an Arminian, believing in the free will of every individual whilst the Evangelicals were mostly moderate Calvinists who believed in the sovereign election of God for salvation. The theological divide was deep and often acrimonious,

Centre: *John Ryle MP, the father of J C Ryle, who lost the family fortune*

Right: Monument to Charles Roe 'Reader, when thou hast performed the duties which brought thee hither, think on the founder of this beautiful edifice.' His monument includes his three great concerns—the silk mill, the erection of Christ Church and the copper smelter in Toxteth Park, Liverpool

Above: Charles Roe (1715–1781) who founded the silk industry in Macclesfield

and expressed in their books and correspondence, and even reflected in their hymns. But there were some who tried to reconcile those who were divided. For example, Bryan Collins, briefly David Simpson's curate, preached for the Arminian John Wesley and the Calvinist Selina the Countess of Huntingdon. It was Collins' desire to unite the two factions: 'I wish to do good unto all. I do not love one and dislike another. I can unite with all who are united to Jesus. I care not for names in the least.'

The family home

John Ryle (1783–1862) J C Ryle's father and the eldest son of John Wesley's supporter, was only in his twenties when he inherited a fortune of a quarter of a million pounds (something like £100,000,000 in today's currency). He became a banker and land and property-owner in and around Macclesfield with an estimated annual income of £15,000 to £20,000. Temperamentally he was an open-hearted, generous person better suited to being a country gentleman than a man of business. He was committed to public service and was the Mayor of Macclesfield from 1809 to 1810 and the MP for

Above: Park House, erected in the 1780s and the home of the Ryle family until they moved to Henbury Hall in 1835

Macclesfield from 1832 to 1837. Politically John Ryle was a moderate liberal reformer, but it is not recorded that he ever took part in parliamentary debates. In 1841 he succeeded John Tollemache as the High Sheriff of Cheshire. In Macclesfield (a town of about 25,000 people) John Ryle was regarded as 'almost king of the place'.

In July 1811 John Ryle married Susanna Hurt (1762–1835), from Alderwaskley Hall, Wirksworth, Derbyshire. She also came from a wealthy landowning family and was a distant relation of the industrialist Richard Arkwright. John and Susanna had a family of four daughters and two sons, the elder of whom, John Charles Ryle, was born in Park House on 10 May 1816. In time his sisters Susan and Caroline married clergymen (both of whom were friends of J C Ryle), late in life, Emma married an army captain, and his eldest sister Mary, remained unmarried. His younger brother Frederick, who remained a bachelor, was ordained and died in his mid-twenties.

Above: Park House, demolished in the early 20th century, was situated on the north side of 'Ryle's Pool'. In 1922 what remained of the original estate was given to the town and renamed South Park

The Ryle family were prosperous and privileged and lived in some style at Park House, Macclesfield. The earliest childhood memory of J C Ryle was of a large black dog taking a biscuit out of his hand. Dogs were to play an important part in his life and the first one he owned was a Lyme Hall mastiff, and he was so attached to the dog that after it died he kept its brass collar. Many of the family summer holidays were spent at Bridlington where John Ryle owned a yacht called *Seaflower*.

Outwardly the Ryle family were socially respectable and nominally religious. On Sundays they attended Christ Church but there were no family prayers at home and Sundays were much like any other day of the week. Out of a sense of duty some members of the family might read the occasional sermon but they were invariably bored and unaffected by them. As a child J C Ryle had read John Bunyan's *Pilgrim's Progress* and Mary Sherwood's *Conversations on the Church Catechism*, and sometimes his mother heard him repeat the Church of England catechism, 'which she did in a very grave and rather gloomy manner'. Later he reflected that as children: 'we had few cares, no sickness, no death, no anxieties and wanted for nothing' but they were 'destitute of any real religion'.

Looking back Ryle was saddened that he had not known his evangelical grandfather, for within the family there was not

Top: Ryle Street, Macclesfield was named after the family
Above left: Bridlington, Yorkshire where members of the Ryle family spent their summer holidays
Above right: Bridlington Priory

Left: *St Michael's church, Macclesfield. J C Ryle maintained that at both St Michael's and Christ Church, 'the clergymen were wretched high and dry sticks of the old school and their preaching was not calculated to do good to anybody.'*

a 'whit of what may be called a real spiritual religion … We sometimes heard rumours when we were children, of certain strange clergymen who were called evangelical, but we never came across any of them; and were sedulously brought up to regard them as well-meaning, extravagant, fanatical enthusiasts, who carried things a great deal too far in religion.' Those clergy who took their faith seriously were regarded with suspicion and considered to be dangerous 'enthusiasts' or 'Methodists'. Later Ryle recalled that 'there were only two churches in Macclesfield. You might have slept as comfortably in those churches under the sermons of their ministers as you

Ryle's Evangelical faith

Looking back to the evangelicalism of the 18th century Ryle saw it as a model for his own day: 'I am bold to say that we want nothing new—no new systems, no new school of teaching, no new theology, no new ceremonial, no new gospel. We want nothing but the old truths, rightly preached and rightly brought home to consciences, minds and wills. The evangelical system of theology revived England a hundred years ago, and I have faith to believe that it could revive it again … The first want of our day is a return to the old, simple and sharply-cut doctrines of our fathers in the last century; and the second want is a generation of like-minded and like-gifted men to preach them.'

Ryle believed that there were four characteristics of evangelicalism: First, 'the inspiration, sufficiency and supremacy of Holy Scripture'. The Bible was the rock and all else was sand. Second, 'the sinfulness, guilt and corruption of human nature'. The fall of Adam resulted in what is known as original sin. Third, 'the work and offices of our Lord Jesus Christ' as our representative, substitute and mediator, who has obtained salvation for us and redemption from sin. Fourth, the work of the Holy Spirit: inwardly, in our hearts and outwardly, in our lives. For Ryle these characteristics provided the 'principal things in Christianity' and 'the leading features of evangelical religion.' For Ryle nothing less than this was consistent with Scripture.

Left: St George's church, where the evangelical minister was John Burnet (1800–1870). On leaving St George's in 1847 he became the vicar of Bradford

might in your own armchairs, with nothing to wake you up.' While Methodism continued to flourish in the town, by the 1820s the evangelicalism of David Simpson was a distant memory.

'Stirring among the dry bones'

In 1830 the Irish evangelical John Burnet was appointed to St George's church and his seventeen-year ministry had a significant impact on the local community. At the time, St George's was an episcopal chapel situated not far from the centre of Macclesfield and which became the parish church of Sutton in 1835. Ryle recorded, 'there came a true preacher of the gospel in the pulpit of that church. The church was called St George in Sutton, and as it stood side by side with a new Wesleyan chapel, the two were called St George and the Dragon ... The result was a stirring among the dry bones. Large congregations gathered together, and people were set talking and thinking about the gospel of Jesus Christ.' Some years later Ryle recalled that he was indebted to John Burnet 'for much of the spiritual

Right: In May 1898 Bishop J C Ryle preached the final sermon in St Michael's before the building was closed for restoration. It reopened in April 1901 in the presence of his son Bishop Herbert Ryle

light and knowledge' that he had received. Ryle's sister Susan started to attend the church and when she became an evangelical she was ridiculed by members of her family, but this sowing of the seed by Burnet was later reaped when Ryle was himself soundly converted in Oxford in 1837.

Early education and Eton

Ryle was taught to read and write by the parish clerk of St Michael's church, and he learnt Latin from his sisters' governess. As a child he loved to read and could always be kept quiet with a book. When he was only eight years old he attended a small private boarding school run by the Rev. John Jackson and attended by the sons of other wealthy Cheshire families. While he gained a thorough grounding in Latin and Greek, he was also bullied, and was happiest during the school holidays when he was with his family. Looking back Ryle didn't think that he was 'an ill-natured, bad-tempered boy, but I was sturdy, very independent and combative. I had a very strong opinion of my own, and never cared a bit for being in a minority, and was ready to fight anybody however big if necessary.' He added, 'I remember when I was a schoolboy I would wake up, however tired with a long journey, when I began to draw near home. Soon as I saw the old hills, and trees, and chimneys, the sense of weariness was gone, and I was all alive. The prospect of soon seeing much-loved faces, the joy of thinking of a family gathering,

Top Right: John Keate (1773–1852) was the headmaster of Eton College for twenty-five years and is known more for his flogging than his teaching
Above: Eton College, Windsor was founded by Henry VI and became one of the leading English public schools

Right: When he
was eighteen years
old Ryle recorded
his personal
measurements:
Height 6' 1$^{7/8}$";
waist 31$^{1/2}$";
length of arm 2' 7";
horizontal reach
of both arms
6' 2$^{1/2}$"; span of
fingers 9$^{1/2}$"; neck
15$^{1/2}$"; across the
shoulders 1' 7"

all this was able to drive sleep
away.' But he hated the return to
school.

Ryle was a typical upper
middle-class Victorian and his
social attitude is reflected in
his comments about education.
Today his views sound snobbish,
but at the time anyone from
his background would have
echoed his words. He believed
that 'a boy's first school is a
turning point in his life.' Parents
should carefully select a good
preparatory school for their sons,
but if they didn't take this first
stage seriously, then such parents
were 'nothing better than short-
sighted, foolish, unintelligent
and senseless geese'. Beyond
the preparatory school it was
expected that the boy would then
be educated at a public school, but

girls would have been educated
at home and were not sent away
to school.

In January 1828 Ryle entered
Eton College, Windsor, and
was put into the house run by
the assistant master Edward
Hawtrey. The boys were mostly
unsupervised, the staff took little
interest in the pupils and fighting
was common. Early on Ryle
had his one and only fight with
the school bully, and admitted
that it took six months to settle
into the school. Initially he was
thoroughly miserable, but later
believed 'that a public school is
about the best discipline that a
boy can be put through, and the
want of it is a great detriment to
a boy all through his life.' From
1809 to 1834 the headmaster of
Eton was the notorious Rev. Dr

John Keate. Though he was an amiable man, a first-rate scholar, a poet and accomplished teacher, by today's standards he was a sadistic bully. Keate enforced the harsh discipline of the school by flogging the boys into submission, some of whom were only six or seven years old. As a pupil Ryle was twice flogged by the headmaster. Once for firing a pistol, and then for being absent when the register was called; a cricket match had finished early and the team went to an inn to celebrate, but when this was discovered the furious Keate beat them all.

Riots in public schools were not uncommon. In 1797 troops had to be sent into Rugby School and the Riot Act read, and at the time the most rebellious school was Harrow. After the last riot took place at Eton in 1832, Keate flogged eighty boys in a single day! In that year the custom of tossing boys in a blanket was banned after a boy was seriously injured—he hit the ceiling and his skull was broken. Alongside all of this Ryle commended the system of 'fagging' (junior boys acting as servants to the older pupils) and believed that it did good to the pupils. This conclusion is unsurprising since in his final year he had eight fags—four boys to wait on him at breakfast and four at tea. Writing in the early 1870s, he considered that 'fagging as it now exists at Eton I believe to be a thoroughly good system' and he also believed that it was right for children to be whipped.

The curriculum at Eton, like that of other public schools at the time, was very limited and little else was taught apart from Latin and Greek; it was Ryle's good memory that helped him to study the classics. There was some teaching of English, history and French but he regretted that 'not one word of arithmetic, algebra or mathematics did I learn the whole seven years I was at Eton.' He studied the Thirty-Nine Articles of Religion when he entered for a Newcastle scholarship.

In addition to his studies Ryle took an active part in the debating society and was a keen sportsman. He took lessons in fencing and enjoyed hockey, rowing and cricket. Rowing was known as 'wet-bobs and cricket 'dry bobs'. He was a member of the Upper Club, from which the first eleven were chosen and in 1834 he became the captain of the cricket team that played

Above: *Like other school boys, Ryle left his mark by carving his name on the panelling in the Upper School. Below it are the names of his sons, Herbert and Arthur*

against Harrow and Winchester. Ryle was a powerful striker and a fast round arm bowler, and because of his height—he was nearly 6' 2" tall—he was given the nickname 'Magnus'. His height and his leadership on the cricket field gave him 'a power of commanding, managing, organising and directing, seeing through men's capacities and using every man in the post to which he is best suited.' These skills proved to be invaluable to him throughout his clerical career.

Whilst at school, Ryle was confirmed, and he received his first communion when he was back at St Michael's church, Macclesfield. The confirmation services were formal—on one occasion Keate flogged all of the candidates!—and no attempt was made to give any spiritual direction to the pupils. Ryle noted that 'religion was at a very low ebb, and most boys knew far more about the heathen gods and goddesses, than about Jesus Christ.' He was first challenged to consider the seriousness of sin from his school friend, and future brother-in-law, Algernon Coote, who rebuked him for swearing.

Looking back on his time at Eton, Ryle later remarked that the Sunday sermons 'were a perfect farce and a disgrace to the Church of England.' The addresses, usually delivered by former clerical masters of the school, were often repeated. One on 'Peter' was preached several times and so was one on the unlikely text 'His mother made him a little coat' (1 Samuel 2:19).

Before Ryle left Eton, the new headmaster, Edward Hawtrey, requested that his portrait should be painted. Herbert Ryle (one of J C Ryle's sons) described the picture as that of 'a well-grown, distinguished looking young-man, fashionably dressed, with thick wavy dark hair, clear complexion and an attractive look of thoughtful dignity.' Looking back on his time at public school, Ryle said 'I left Eton with unfeigned regret', having experienced 'one of the happiest periods of my life'.

Back in Cheshire during the school holidays Ryle was never idle. He read widely, spent time with his two Lyme Hall mastiffs, and engaged 'in fishing, boating, carpentry, shooting, occasionally riding, cutting down trees, or some violent exercises.' When the weather was bad he read 'an enormous quantity of miscellaneous literature in my father's library' and when visitors stayed with his parents at Park House he enjoyed playing cards and dancing. 'I was always passionately fond of dancing from the time I was fifteen and especially fancied waltzing, reels, country dances, Sir Roger de Coverley, and anything that had steam and life and go in it.' Overall, his life was worldly, secure and self-contained. Later, after his conversion, he concluded that races, balls, operas, theatres and card-parties were 'all very doubtful methods of spending time.'

TRAVEL INFORMATION

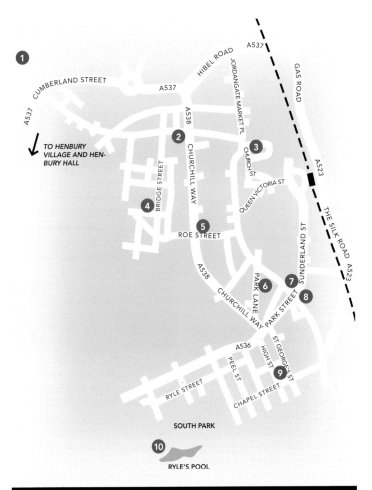

MAP OF MACCLESFIELD

KEY
1 West Park Museum
2 Chestergate House
  (Charles Roe's House)
3 St Michael's Church
4 Christ Church
5 Heritage Centre
6 Silk Museum
7 Site of Ryle's Bank
8 John Ryle's House
9 St George's Chambers
10 Site of Park House

Macclesfield is situated off the M6, exit at junction 19, and then follow the A556 and A537. The town contains several fine 18th century buildings and a number of former silk mills. From the rail station the town centre is easily accessible.

Above: *The Regency Silk Mill, Macclesfield one of several such mills in the town*

TOURIST INFORMATION

Tourist Information Centre, Town Hall, Macclesfield SK10 1DX
www.macclesfield@cheshireeast.gov.uk
✆ 01625 504 114

Macclesfield museums

Silk Industry Museum, Park Lane, Macclesfield SK11 6TJ
www.spinningtheweb.org.uk/collections5.php
✆ 01625 612 045

The building was once the Macclesfield School of Art. The museum is open from 11.00am to 5.00pm Monday to Saturday and closed on Sunday. Tickets are available from the museum for conducted tours around the nearby Paradise Mill containing twenty-six restored hand-looms. During the summer months the tours are at 12.15pm, 1.30pm and 2.45pm.

The Heritage Centre, Roe Street, Macclesfield SK11 6UT
✆ 01625 613 210

This museum tells the story of the silk industry in Macclesfield. The Heritage Centre is open from 11.00am to

Above: *The Heritage Centre, in a former Sunday School erected in 1813 and opened in 1814*

5.00pm Monday to Saturday and closed on Sunday. There is an informative presentation on the silk industry, gift shop and The Mulberry Tree Coffee Shop
✆ 01625 619 909.

West Park Museum, Prestbury Road, Macclesfield SK10 3BJ
✆ 01625 613 210 (and during opening hours ✆ 01625 619 831)
The small museum contains Egyptian artefacts, and displays on the artist Charles Tunnicliffe and the industrialist, Charles Roe. Closed on Monday, but otherwise open from 1.30–4.30pm, and admission is free.

Left: From 1753 to 1781 Chestergate House was the home of Charles Roe

St George's, church, St George's Place, Macclesfield

The building was opened in 1823 as an Independent chapel and reopened in 1828 as an episcopal chapel and was consecrated by the Bishop of Chester in July 1834. In the following year it became the parish church of nearby Sutton. The second Anglican minister, John Burnet, appointed in 1830, was responsible for the erection of St James church, more suitably located in the village

St Michael and All Angel's church, Church Street, Macclesfield

www.stmichaels-macclesfield.com

St Michael's, originally a chapel in the large parish of Prestbury, was rebuilt on the same site and became a parish church in 1835. In the north aisle is a memorial tablet to J C Ryle. In recent years the church has been re-ordered and a welcome area created containing meeting rooms, kitchen and toilets. In the Savage Chapel is a Geneva Bible.

Christ Church (access from Bridge Street), Macclesfield

The Churches Conservation Trust www.visitchurches.org.uk

Christ Church opened as a private chapel in December 1775 and was consecrated by the Bishop of Chester in December 1779. It contains the Ryle family pew and fine monuments to David Simpson and Charles Roe. It became a parish church in 1888, but after the congregation declined it closed in 1981 and is now under the care of The Churches Conservation Trust. From April to September the building is open between 10.00am to 3.00pm, Monday, Tuesday and Friday; and from October to March only on Monday. However when it is closed access may be obtained from Tim Brinton
✆ 01625 423 894.

Above: Christ Church, Macclesfield was a place of worship for 200 years

of Sutton. St George's church, which closed in 1999 was converted into offices and reopened in 2004 as St George's Chambers. Inside the entrance lobby is a wall tablet to John Ryle MP. The building is not open to the public.

Above: The interior of St Michael's church, Macclesfield

❷ What does the future hold?

At Oxford, Ryle was soundly converted to faith in Christ, and having gained a good degree could have become an academic, a lawyer, a banker, or member of parliament. Instead, the trauma of his father's bankruptcy brought him to ordination in the Church of England

In the 1830s the University of Oxford consisted of small, independent college communities each of between 100 to 200 male students, tutors and chaplains. Most of the students were destined for the professions, and particularly as clergy in the Church of England. In October 1834 Ryle became a student at Christ Church, a college with the largest quadrangle in Oxford, and where the chapel serves as the cathedral for the diocese of Oxford. Ryle was awarded an exhibition and a scholarship and after three years study graduated with a first class degree in classics.

He believed that if he had been better supervised by his tutors he would not have wasted his first two years, but he made up for this by working much harder in his third year. Part of the final examination was held in public and the candidates had to answer questions on any topic the examiners cared to ask, particularly in divinity. 'When my own turn came, I came off with flying colours and answered every question put to me with perfect ease, because as luck would have it, they did not ask me anything I did not know perfectly.' He was congratulated by the examiners,

and awarded a first class BA in February 1838 but, unusually, did not proceed to MA until June 1871.

Given his academic record Ryle could have remained at Oxford as a university teacher but he declined to do so and only returned many years later when he was invited to preach before the university. As a student he was also expected to pass a basic examination on the Bible, the Thirty-Nine Articles of Religion, the Book of Common Prayer and church history. This

Above: *The Divinity School, Oxford*

Facing Page: *J C Ryle was a student at Christ Church, Oxford*

was the only formal theological education he had before he was ordained, which meant that most of his theological reading was delayed until he was in parish ministry.

As well as his studies at university Ryle continued to be involved in sport and was the captain of the first eleven cricket team, and one of those who helped to revive cricket matches between Oxford and Cambridge. Though he was a good bowler, he was only a modest batsman and his highest score was fourteen runs. During the summer he was obsessed with cricket and played from noon to dusk every day of the week. Apart from sport, Ryle lived a rather solitary existence and concluded that he disliked the university and wished to see it reformed. Although he came from a very privileged background he reacted against the worldly lives of many of his fellow undergraduates: 'Nothing disgusted me so much as the miserable idolatry of money and also of aristocratic connection. I never saw such an amount of toadying flattery, and fawning upon wealth and title as I saw among the undergraduates at Oxford.'

Though Ryle's *Autobiography* was only intended to be read by members of his family, his words had a wider application: 'the advice I give to all young men who go to university is, to begin from the very first the habit of regular reading,

The Oxford Movement

Ryle was at Oxford when a small group of clerical intellectuals attempted to change the face of the Church of England. They were romantics who looked nostalgically back to the Middle Ages. The teaching of the early church fathers shaped their thinking and they were dismissive of the 16th century Protestant Reformation. They felt that the Church of England was being side-lined by the state, particularly when the secular powers attempted to interfere with the church and its administration. The main leaders of what became known as the Oxford Movement were John Henry Newman (1801–1890), John Keble (1792–1866) and Edward Bouverie Pusey (1800–1882). While the last two remained in the Church of England, Newman followed the logic of his position and was one of 450 or so clergy who became Roman Catholics. Ryle was highly critical of the Movement and considered it to be both a dangerous influence and evidence of 'the deep corruption of man's heart' in craving for 'sensual, carnal worship.'

Between 1833 and 1841 ninety *Tracts for the Times* were published and they set out the principles of the Movement. These documents were dismissed by evangelicals, and when Newman tried to give a catholic interpretation of the Thirty-Nine Articles of the Church of England, the series ended amidst widespread condemnation. Initially catholic teaching was adopted by only a minority of clergy and laity, but by the 1850s and 1860s it had become more widespread and had developed into Anglo-Catholicism. Throughout his ministry in Suffolk and Liverpool Ryle was deeply opposed to ritualistic practice and its doctrinal teaching.

Below right: *John Henry Newman, who wrote twenty-four of the* Tracts for the Times, *left the Church of England in 1845 and became a Roman Catholic. For Ryle, his 'migration was one more proof that ritualism is the highway to Rome'*

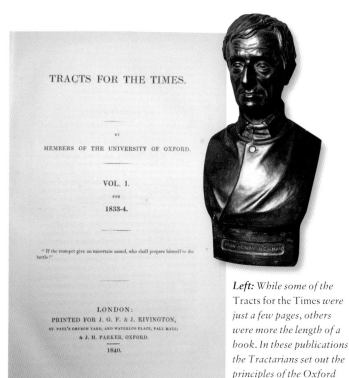

Left: *While some of the* Tracts for the Times *were just a few pages, others were more the length of a book. In these publications the Tractarians set out the principles of the Oxford Movement*

and to beware of dawdling away time in objectless, purposeless, mischievous ways [for] it is astonishing how much time an undergraduate may waste if he does not take care.'

Personal faith

It was during his final year at Oxford that Ryle was soundly converted to faith in Christ. He confessed that between the ages of seven and twenty-one he had never prayed, read the Bible or held any religious convictions. Yet unlike many of his university contemporaries, Ryle had not fallen into immorality, drunkenness, gambling, horse-racing or gone to the theatre—at that time considered to be a serious sin by evangelicals. For several months in the midsummer of 1837 he was unwell and this crisis—the first of many in his life—challenged him to read his Bible and to pray. It became his life-long practice to read the Old and New Testaments and once completed to begin again.

One Sunday, after the service had started, Ryle wandered into an Oxford church. He was nearing

Left: From 1835 to 1841 the Ryle family lived at Henbury Hall near Macclesfield.
J C Ryle commented, 'When we lived there, there was much that was extremely beautiful about it both in the grounds and the distant views from them, and I soon became exceedingly attached to it'

his final examination and was feeling depressed. As he entered the building the second lesson from Ephesians 2 was being read, and the reader made some lengthy pauses as he read verse 8: 'By grace—are ye saved—through faith—and that not of yourselves—it is the gift of God.' The words struck home to Ryle's heart, and led to his conversion. By the beginning of the following year Ryle knew that 'I was fairly launched as a Christian, and started on a road which I think I have never entirely left from that time to this.' His grasp of the truth meant that he had 'become alive and had a hope of heaven'. His Christian faith, which was deeply rooted in Christ, was able to sustain him through the humiliating loss of the family fortune, and later during the illness and death of his two wives and a daughter. However his family, and particularly his cousin the Rev. John Ryle Wood, the vicar of St John's church, Worcester, was horrified by his evangelical conversion.

Right: 6 Stone Buildings, Lincoln's Inn, London where J C Ryle considered embarking on a legal career

Above: The Oxford and Cambridge University Club was founded in 1830 and
71 Pall Mall was opened in 1838

Right: St John's Chapel, Bedford Row was one of the leading proprietary chapels
in London and had a succession of evangelical ministers. The building, which
was erected in the 18th century, was demolished in 1863

London interlude

In 1835 when Ryle was away
at Oxford his father bought
Henbury Hall, three miles west of
Macclesfield. It cost him £55,000
and it was a fitting residence for
a gentleman-banker. The estate
consisted of about 1,000 acres
and during the vacations J C Ryle
became increasingly attached to
the property.

Within a year after leaving
Oxford he went to Lincoln's Inn,
London to try his hand at law to
see if it suited him. He entered
the chambers of the colourful
Jonathan Christie who, in 1821,
had been tried and acquitted at the
Old Bailey for the death of a man
in a duel. Ryle had lodgings in Pall
Mall and became a member of
the Oxford and Cambridge Club.

In London he appears to have
spent time with what he described
as 'worldly companions', but
on Sundays he attended the
fashionable St John's Chapel,
Bedford Row, Bloomsbury.
The minister was the celebrated
preacher, Baptist Noel, who on
leaving the Church of England in
1848, became a Baptist pastor.

From riches to poverty

Ryle spent eighteen months in London, but after becoming unwell he returned to Cheshire and soon adopted the lifestyle of a provincial gentleman. He entered the family bank, became a county magistrate and a Captain of the Macclesfield Troop of the Cheshire Yeomanry. This volunteer force was called out to keep the peace, and each year the men marched to Liverpool for exercises on the Crosby Sands. Soon Ryle was invited to speak at religious and political meetings, and there was every expectation that he might enter parliament. He continued to play cricket and took part in gentlemen's matches with other counties. At Henbury Hall he led family prayers in the housekeeper's room for two female servants but other members of the family never came.

Coming from such a well-connected county family, Ryle spent time in the company of other wealthy families and inevitably met a number of young ladies whom his parents considered to be potential wives for their son. But he felt ill at ease with women, and confessed

Above: The Cheshire Yeomanry in which Ryle held the rank of captain

that 'unfortunately I did not feel the least inclination to marry them.' Had he married, his father would have given him £800 a year and a house, and as the eldest son he would have inherited Henbury Hall and a large fortune. He later reflected that 'I can see clearly that it was a period in which God was fitting me for after-work in a way I did not know.'

Poignantly, in his later tracts (see chapter 6 for his tract writing) Ryle made occasional references to banks and banknotes, for example: 'the banknote without a signature at the bottom is nothing but a worthless piece of paper. The stroke of a pen confers on it all its value.' But in July 1841 neither banknote nor signature was of any particular significance when the Macclesfield and Cheshire Bank ceased to trade, the London bank that was the guarantor stopped payment and John Ryle was made bankrupt. He who had so much material wealth lost it all in a matter of weeks. He was obliged to sell his three estates at Henbury, Upton (near Macclesfield) and Errwood

Above: The site of the Macclesfield and Cheshire Bank (later the Post Office) in Park Green, Macclesfield, is now the Bathstore. The building on the right was the home of J C Ryle's grandfather

Above: After the collapse of the Macclesfield and Cheshire Bank the building became the Post Office

(near Buxton), and to dismiss the thirteen resident servants at Henbury Hall (and others who lived in the locality), and J C Ryle, his sister Mary and their parents spent six weeks sorting out their possessions, and took with them their furniture, bookcases for 1,000 books, paintings and engravings, silver, glass and china.

All that J C Ryle ended up with was £250 from the sale of his two horses, his yeomanry uniform, sword and saddlery. He was particularly devastated over losing his Lyme Hall mastiff, Caesar. The dog was given away but, unloved, it soon died. Throughout his life Ryle loved dogs and the separation from Caesar was a painful experience. Looking back to this period of his life he confessed, 'I do not think there has been a single day in my life for thirty-two years, that I have not remembered the faint humiliation of having to leave Henbury ... nothing has made me forget my sudden violent expulsion from Cheshire in [August] 1841.' Within a matter of months J C Ryle had lost his home and his inheritance: 'We got up one summer's morning with all the world before us as usual, and went to bed that same night completely and entirely ruined.'

The Macclesfield and Cheshire Bank

The Macclesfield and Cheshire bank of Daintry and Ryle was founded in 1810. The bank prospered and in 1821 the then partners, John Smith Daintry and John Ryle opened another bank in Manchester, the too much capital, and thousands of pounds were lost. From 1836 Ryle wanted to close the Manchester bank, but Ravenscroft refused to do so. Three years later Ryle was desperate. 'I cannot tell you how miserable I am under these circumstances' and he confessed that he was at to have had a penny, and the result was my father's ruin.'

Once the Manchester bank had collapsed it brought down with it the parent bank in Macclesfield. Ryle and Daintry were declared bankrupt with a total debt of £225,000 (about ten million pounds in today's currency). As J C Ryle understood the situation, his father's income had been about £15,000 to £20,000 a year, and the loss on the property was in the region of £500,000 to £600,000. John and Susanna Ryle cut their losses and moved to Hampshire and lived off the interest derived from her private income. J C Ryle concluded that his 'father was never fit to be a banker. He was too easy going, too good natured and too careless about details.'

Above: A banknote signed by J C Ryle

management of which was in the hands of partners—Samuel Bayley (until 1832) and William Ravenscroft (until 1840). Unfortunately Ravenscroft was prepared to advance his 'wit's end' about the situation. As J C Ryle saw it, 'the funds of the bank were squandered away by hundreds of thousands, by loans and advances to people who ought never

Right: From 1841 to 1862, 1 Eastern Terrace (now part of Bramley House) Crescent Road, Anglesea, was the home of the Ryle family, and after John Ryle's death the house and its contents were sold

Above: *The high churchman Samuel Wilberforce (1805–1873) was the rector of St Mary's, Alverstoke from 1841 to 1844, and his preaching attracted large congregations particularly of naval officers. His wife Emily died shortly after they moved to Alverstoke*

A new home for the family

However, the Ryle family were certainly not destitute, and their changed circumstances can be greatly exaggerated. Socially they may have come down in the world, but they were nowhere near as poor as many of J C Ryle's future parishioners. Though his father may have been made bankrupt, his mother still had her own private fortune of £30,000, and this provided for herself, her husband and their two unmarried daughters, Mary and Emma. The family settled in Anglesey Ville (now called Anglesey); described as a prosperous 'new watering place' in the parish of Alverstoke, to the west of the growing town of Gosport. The hamlet of Anglesey became an attractive location for the gentry and nobility who came to enjoy the benefits of sea-bathing and the local amenities: a reading room, bath house and gardens.

The Ryle family lived in a well furnished house in Eastern Terrace, in what is now called Crescent Road, where they had a housekeeper and three servants. They had moved to Hampshire to be near to Frederick who was, in the opinion of J C Ryle, his mother's favourite son. Frederick was four years younger than John and followed him to Eton College and Christ Church, Oxford. Temperamentally they were very different, and Ryle described his brother as being 'an exceedingly gentle, quiet, undemonstrative person, and never acted or spoke strongly about anybody or anything, and was a most blameless amiable fellow … He walked steadily on his own way, and I rushed on impetuously in my own, and this was the case till he died.' Frederick was ordained to a fellowship at Brasenose College, Oxford before becoming one of Samuel Wilberforce's curates. Coolness developed between the two brothers and J C Ryle believed that they could never be at one when they did not agree over 'what was true religion.' Clearly Frederick did not share his older brother's evangelical convictions.

Samuel Wilberforce, the third son of the anti-slave campaigner, was the archdeacon of Surrey (attached to a canonry at Winchester cathedral) and rector of Alverstoke. Later he was briefly the Dean of Westminster, before becoming the Bishop of Oxford in November 1846. After J C Ryle had been ordained Wilberforce occasionally invited him to preach at Alverstoke. Inwardly Ryle was contemptuous of him. He believed that Wilberforce, a high churchman, secretly disliked him—probably because of his fervent evangelicalism—and regarded

Above: John Ryle (J C Ryle's father) died at 11 Leam Terrace, Leamington Spa and his body was interred in the town cemetery

Below: Memorial tablet to John Ryle in the entrance lobby of St George's church, now St. George's Chambers, Macclesfield

IN MEMORY OF
JOHN RYLE ESQ.RE OF PARK HOUSE MACCLESFIELD
ONE OF THE FIRST MEMBERS OF PARLIAMENT
FOR THIS BOROUGH.

DIED AT LEAMINGTON APRIL 22ND 1862,
AGED 79 YEARS.

THIS TABLET WAS ERECTED AS A SMALL TOKEN
OF RESPECT BY ONE OF HIS OLD SERVANTS.

Above: St Thomas' church, Elson, was consecrated on 14 August 1845 and the first minister was Frederick Ryle, J C Ryle's younger brother

him as a dangerous individual, and Ryle was concerned that Wilberforce exercised an 'extremely pernicious' influence over members of his family, particularly his mother, his brother Frederick and sister Mary, but not, it would appear, over his father. Of greater concern (had he known about it) was his sister Emma's correspondence with Henry Manning (then a high churchman and later a Roman Catholic cardinal).

In the extensive parish of Alverstoke there were three Anglican churches and Wilberforce was responsible for the erection of two more—St Matthew's, Gosport and St Thomas', Elson—and in 1845 Wilberforce appointed Frederick Ryle to become the first minister of the chapel of ease at Elson. But in May 1846 when he was aged only twenty-six, Frederick died

of 'peritonitis from constipation' a condition that had already brought about the death of his uncle Thomas. Frederick's body was interred in Elson churchyard, and in June 1849 the local National school was opened in his memory. This school closed in 1967.

Susanna Ryle died of bowel cancer in April 1852 and was interred next to Frederick. Ten years later John Ryle died unexpectedly while he was staying in Leamington Spa. His gravestone simply records that he was 'sometime MP for Macclesfield' and includes texts (presumably chosen by his son) that refer to being awake and not asleep (Mark 13:35–37) and the beatitude, 'blessed are the peacemakers' (Matthew 5:9). The death certificate described him as a 'landed proprietor' and given all that had happened nineteen

Above: *New Park, Lyndhurst, the home of William Thornhill, is now the New Park Manor Hotel*

years before, it is ironic that the word 'banker' was crossed out. All that remained of the family fortune was under £600, and it was equally divided between his two unmarried daughters Mary and Emma. Yet his son and heir received nothing.

Personal reflection

To have lost everything was a terrible disgrace to the family, and Ryle confessed that if he had not been a Christian, he might have committed suicide. Outwardly he appeared calm and contented, but inwardly he was bitterly disappointed. 'God alone knows how the iron entered into my soul and how my whole frame, body, mind and spirit reeled and were shaken to the foundation, under the blow of my father's ruin.' It was 'a very bitter cup', and years later he admitted 'it did crush me terribly and for many years I could hardly lift up my head.' He felt ashamed, cut off from his own

social class, and throughout his life, day after day he 'remembered the faint humiliation of having to leave Henbury.'

Ryle's immediate response was to run away to some distant part of England where he was unknown and where he could begin again. Initially he stayed with an uncle in London, and then he and his sister Emma stayed for three months with Lieut-Colonel William Thornhill and his sister Mary. Thornhill was the deputy surveyor of the New Forest and they lived at their imposing home, New Park, Lyndhurst. As Ryle considered what to do next he concluded that 'this ends the bleakest chapter of my life … I believe that God never expects us to feel no suffering or pain when it pleases him to visit us with affliction … to feel trouble deeply and yet submit to it patiently is that which is required of a Christian.'

TRAVEL INFORMATION

MAP OF ALVERSTOKE

KEY
1   St Mary's Church,
    Alverstoke
2   Site of St Mark's Church
3   John Ryle's house
4   Regency Ornamental
    Gardens

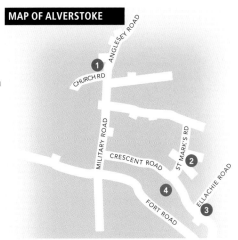

Henbury Hall and Gardens

Henbury Hall,
Macclesfield SK11 9PJ
www.henbury.hall
© 01625 422 101

The Henbury Hall estate is situated about three miles west of Macclesfield off the A537. John Ryle bought the 18th century house for £55,000, and his family lived there from 1835 to 1841. The following year the Hall was acquired by Thomas Mashall, who erected St Thomas' church in the nearby village of Henbury. The Hall was demolished in 1957 and replaced by a superb Palladian style house set within a twelve acre landscaped garden, and is considered to be one of the most beautiful houses in Cheshire. The house and gardens are not open to the public, but once a year the garden is open for the National Gardens Scheme.

Above: *The new Henbury Hall, designed by Julian Bicknell was completed in 1986*

Jodrell Bank

Jodrell Bank Visitor Centre and Arboretum, Macclesfield, Cheshire SK11 9DL
www.manchester.ac.uk/ jodrellbank/viscen
© 01477 571 339

Jodrell Bank is about six miles from junction 18 of the M6, on the A535 between Holmes Chapel and Alderley Edge. There are a number of visitor attractions including the Lovell Telescope (completed in 1957), a 3D theatre, the thirty-five acre Arboretum containing 2,000 species of trees and shrubs, and a visitor shop, café and picnic area. The usual opening hours are from 10.30am to 5.00pm.

❸ Isolation in the New Forest

J C Ryle began his ordained ministry in Exbury in the New Forest. After two years he was exhausted and went for medical treatment at Leamington Spa before his appointment as rector of the largest parish in Winchester

Following the family misfortune Ryle knew that he would have to make his own way in the world, and he considered his options. To become a civil engineer or lawyer would not provide much income for several years, and the thought of being a private tutor did not appeal to him. He even contemplated becoming a secretary to the politician, William Gladstone. Although Ryle disliked the idea of being ordained, he knew that it would at least give him independence and a regular, if modest, income. Neither of Ryle's parents liked the idea of their eldest son becoming a clergyman, but since they could suggest nothing else, with a heavy heart he accepted the situation. As Ryle considered his future he was unexpectedly offered a curacy by William Gibson, the evangelical rector of Fawley. Gibson, 'a most earnest clergyman' was, in Ryle's opinion, dominated by his wife who believed Ryle to be 'a dangerous, extreme man'. The parish was situated in the diocese of Winchester, and Ryle would have approached the bishop concerning his ordination.

On 12 December 1841 Ryle was made a deacon in the chapel of Farnham Castle by Charles Sumner, and a year later he was ordained priest on 11 December. He was appointed as curate of St Katherine's, Exbury, a chapel of ease in the parish of Fawley. In 1841 the scattered district of Exbury consisted of 3,066 acres with a population of 406 people. Ryle received a modest stipend of £100 a year, and lived in the nearby hamlet of Langley, where he had a maid-servant, a boy, a dog, a cat and a pig. The maid was dishonest, and she married the boy who was thirteen years her junior. Both the cat and the pig died, but

Above: *Charles Sumner was the Bishop of Winchester from 1827 to 1869*

Facing Page: *The New Forest, Hampshire*

Charles Sumner (1790–1874)

Charles Richard Sumner was a member of the extended and interconnected Thornton and Wilberforce families. Clerical preferment came quickly to Sumner particularly after receiving the patronage of George IV. In 1824 Sumner became the Bishop of Llandaff and Dean of St Paul's Cathedral, and by 1827 he had been translated to the larger and more prestigious diocese of Winchester. During his forty-year episcopate he improved the diocesan administration and 200 new churches were opened. He was a punctilious time-keeper and prolific letter-writer. He was also a keen supporter of the evangelical Church Missionary Society and the first bishop to preach the annual sermon to the supporters of the Society. Like his brother, John Bird Sumner who was Archbishop of Canterbury from 1848 to 1862, Charles was an evangelical.

Those men who were preparing for ordination by Charles Sumner stayed either at Farnham Castle or in lodgings in the nearby town and for five days they were examined for six hours a day by two examining chaplains; they also had an interview with the bishop who urged each candidate to preach Christ: 'preach him again, preach nothing but Christ'. The ordination service took place in the chapel in Farnham Castle, a venue the bishop much preferred to Winchester Cathedral. After the candidates were ordained the bishop kept closely in touch with each of the men who served in his diocese.

Above: Farnham Castle, the former residence of the bishops of Winchester

EXBURY CHURCH, IN THE NEW FOREST, HANTS—THE CHURCH OF THE REV. J. C. RYLE'S FIRST CURACY.

Above: St Katherine's church, Exbury where Ryle was the curate from 1841 to 1843. Since there was no organ he provided a flute to accompany the singing

fortunately the dog, given Ryle's love of the animal, survived.

Situated near to the church was Exbury House, one of the two manors in the parish. Between 1718 and 1879 it was owned by the aristocratic Mitford family—from whom were descended the notorious 'Mitford sisters' (Jessica became a communist and Diana, a committed fascist, was the second wife of Sir Oswald Mosley). William Mitford (1744–1827) the historian of ancient Greece and an MP, who lived at Exbury House had been responsible for the erection of a model village in Upper Exbury. The houses and church were all built from the distinctive local yellow brick. In his *Autobiography* Ryle made no reference to the

Above: Typical yellow brick houses in Exbury village

Above: St Katherine's church, Exbury, became a separate parish in 1863. The new building was opened in 1908

Above: Catherine Marsh (1818–1912) was a popular writer and philanthropist who provided tracts for the troops in the Crimea War. In 1841 a friend wrote to her: 'John Ryle will be ordained on 12 December and preaches his first sermon on the 19th: would your dear father remember him in prayer?'

'A very dreary, desolate, solitary place'

During Ryle's ministry Exbury church was a plain, rectangular brick structure, with a bell-turret, west gallery with its own fireplace (for the Mitford family), and a three-decker pulpit on the south wall. Of the 170 seats, 150 were free. The building had been consecrated in August 1827, and after being rebuilt was reopened in January 1908. For the new church, members of the Ryle family presented a new pulpit that included their father's favoured preacher's text, 'Woe is unto me, if I preach not the gospel' (1 Corinthians 9:16). The same text is also painted on the wall inside Helmingham church, and is carved into the pulpits at Stradbroke and St Andrew's, Aigburth, Liverpool.

Every Sunday Ryle preached at the morning and afternoon services at Exbury and during the week delivered two biblical addresses in cottages. He also visited his parishioners and gave out tracts, but his personal circumstances meant that he could not give them away but only loan them. These tracts he obtained from the Religious Tract Society in Southampton; but later in Suffolk he wrote his own. He visited each family at least once a month, and as well as performing his clerical duties Ryle provided rudimentary medical care to those who were sick. Although this would have been very basic, it was probably better than nothing at all. He said that he cured cases of ague by administering 'an emetic of ipec[ac] and syrup and afterwards tinct[ure] of quinine.'

Mitfords, and actually implied that there were no gentry living in the area. Perhaps this was an oversight on his part, or that the Mitfords were indifferent to their firebrand evangelical curate. It could be that having experienced the family bankruptcy Ryle felt too vulnerable to associate with people from a similar social background. However, this was no problem to him when he moved to Helmingham when he freely associated with the Tollemache family, and who shared his evangelical convictions.

Left: The Jephson Gardens and monument in Leamington Spa

Below: Henry Jephson was known as 'the father of Leamington Spa'

He administered beef tea to those with scarlet fever, port wine to those who had typhus and olive oil for viper bites. Snakes were common in the area and a local landowner paid 2d for every snake that was killed.

Today Exbury is a small village on the edge of the New Forest and known only for the famous Exbury Gardens. When Ryle lived there he described it as 'a very dreary, desolate, solitary place' consisting of numerous commons, heaths and woodlands. The climate was unhealthy and he never knew a time when 'ague, scarlet fever and typhus' were not found among his parishioners. He remarked that 'drunkenness and sin of every kind abounded' and the area was known for its poachers and smugglers, most of whom were indifferent to religion; those with any faith were mostly Baptists or Methodists. Positively, however, one little girl learnt seventy Bible verses every week.

The inhabitants of Exbury were mostly agricultural labourers, chiefly engaged in growing wheat and barley. Ryle considered the farmers to be 'a rich, dull, stupid set of people' and the labourers as being very neglectful of spiritual matters. The backward nature of the community was evident in the marriage register, where of the four weddings that he conducted, three of the bridegrooms were illiterate, and made their mark instead of signing their names. For their part, the parishioners considered Ryle to be 'an over enthusiastic, fanatical mad dog' and someone to be feared. Yet his great height came in useful when he broke up a fight between two men watched by a crowd of two to three hundred. One individual complained to the bishop when Ryle spoke out against cricket matches ending late on Saturday evenings.

Dr Henry Jephson (1798–1878)

From 1819 Henry Jephson of Leamington Spa became a celebrated physician, and his patients included George IV, Princess Victoria, Florence Nightingale, John Ruskin and William Gladstone. Jephson's treatments brought an increasing number of visitors and residents to the town where he was also a generous benefactor. In July 1814 he officially opened 'The Royal Pump Room and Baths' at a cost of £30,000. Sadly, in 1848 he went blind and a year later a circular structure containing his statue was erected in the renamed Jephson Gardens.

In November 1843 Ryle spent a month under Jephson's supervision, for which only a modest fee was

paid. Jephson's rigorous treatment consisted of a plain diet with plenty of rest and exercise. In itself this would have been sufficient for his exhausted patient, but Ryle also referred to taking 'blue pills to begin with for a week, and then sulphuric acid, dandelion, Leamington waters, and frequent cold shower baths … For diet he allowed neither wine, beer, nor spirits, in fact, nothing but water. No vegetables, pastry, puddings, or cheese, or fruit. Nothing, in short, but mutton chops at 1.30pm and again at 6.30pm, with a little boiled rice, and not a drop of anything to drink from 6.30pm to bedtime.' How effective this treatment was is hard to assess, but at least Ryle survived to tell the tale!

Centre: The Jephson Gardens medal of May 1846

These impressions must have alienated Ryle from those around him, and he observed that 'my residence of two years as curate was not a very cheerful one'. Perhaps in his own mind he had made it out to be more of a 'solitary place' than it actually was. He felt sorry for himself because he had come down in the world and was isolated from those of a similar social background. But apart from his personal feelings he had learnt much about human nature and communicating with the rural poor—lessons that were to become invaluable to him in the years ahead.

Given his own state of mind and with the constant demands upon him, it is not surprising that after two years of sacrificial parochial ministry Ryle was physically exhausted and his own health began to deteriorate. He resigned in November 1843. To recuperate he spent a month in Leamington Spa where he received a rigorous course of treatment from the celebrated physician Dr Henry Jephson, and stayed with Henry Bradley in Clarendon Place. Bradley was a man of some substance with a house at Fawley and a yacht on Southampton water and whose wife attended Exbury church. In Leamington Spa Ryle probably worshipped at St Mary's church

where his friend William Marsh was the incumbent. Over the years the families kept in touch. As late as May 1895 Catherine Marsh still remembered Ryle's birthday, to which he warmly responded: 'you were one of the few remaining friends who remember the birthday of an old man of 79. My recollection of Leamington, of your father and the pleasant little gatherings under his roof [at Lansdowne House] is still fresh and green.'

In the centre of Leamington Spa are the attractive Jephson Gardens which have received several prestigious awards. In the Gardens is the monument to Dr Henry Jephson, and across the road is the Royal Pump Room (much as it would have been known to Ryle) and Art Gallery, Museum, Library and tearoom. About half a mile from the town centre is St Mary's church and nearby the town cemetery where his father is interred.

Winchester interlude

On leaving the New Forest, Ryle wrote *A minster's parting words to the inhabitants of Exbury* and a copy of which was distributed to all seventy-five houses in the district. Shortly after, in November 1843, he became the incumbent of the largest parish in Winchester, and took up his duties the following month. The parish of St Thomas, united with St Clement, had a population of 2,226 and with another 845 soldiers in the nearby barracks. Now Ryle had an annual stipend of £100 together with a house provided for him. The previous rector who was also an evangelical had become progressively inactive, but under Ryle's ministry things immediately changed. Soon the church, which seated 600 people, was filled to capacity, and he began to hold a mid-week Bible exposition in the schoolroom. Typical of the time, fewer people

Left: *St Mary's church, Leamington Spa where William Marsh (1775–1864) was the incumbent from 1843 to 1851. He was a gracious evangelical who was committed to the conversion of the Jews and to the expected imminent second coming of Christ*

attended Holy Communion; the number of communicants being between sixty-four and ninety-three.

Whatever private opinion Ryle might have had of Samuel Wilberforce, the archdeacon showed the new incumbent some kindness when he was staying in Winchester in connection with his cathedral duties. Wilberforce occasionally attended St Thomas' church, and on one occasion late into the night tried to change Ryle's views about baptismal regeneration. Ryle was, however, unmoved by the silver-tongued Wilberforce. For Ryle baptism and regeneration were separate issues. Biblical regeneration was not about ecclesiastical privilege—but about being born again by the Holy Spirit. However this discussion and his residence in Winchester was a mere diversion. Ryle only remained there for just over two months before moving from Hampshire to Suffolk where he was to spend the next thirty-six years.

Ryle the preacher

Looking back to his preaching at Exbury, 'nobody ever told me what was right or wrong in the pulpit. The result was that the first year of my preaching was a series of experiments.' At Winchester his preaching 'consisted entirely of written sermons, of a style I should not care to preach now, because

Above: *Samuel Wilberforce (1805–1873) the third son of William Wilberforce, the anti-slave campaigner, was 'a high churchman from the first.' He was the Bishop of Oxford from 1846 and the Bishop of Winchester from 1869*

they were far too florid, and far less simple and direct than I afterwards learned to preach.' Initially he modelled himself on the eloquent Henry Melville of St Paul's Cathedral, but however appropriate this was for a London congregation it was inappropriate in a rural setting. Ryle soon discovered that he had to 'crucify his style' to communicate with his hearers and became convinced that clergy needed to preach 'with eloquence, life, plainness and power.'

Ryle's sermons were biblical and gospel-centred, containing the 'two simple truths' of repentance and faith. His preparation was thorough and it took a great deal out of him, and his sermons were delivered with passion and conviction. He was all too aware of the gulf between the preacher and his congregation: 'When I stand in a pulpit to preach to a country congregation, it is very much like standing on the battlements of Norwich castle and trying to make myself heard in Norwich cathedral, the distance is so great. If they only hear a noise it is almost all, I fear, that many of them do hear.' He greatly valued expository preaching when people took their Bibles to church 'and compare what they have heard with the written word' and he personally appreciated reading the sermons of the Baptist preacher Charles Haddon Spurgeon.

From his own experience Ryle knew that it was difficult to preach to farmers and farm labourers: 'so far as concerns language and composition, I deliberately say that I would rather preach before the University at Oxford or Cambridge, or the Temple [Church], or Lincoln's Inn, or the Houses of Parliament, than I would address an agricultural congregation on a fine hot afternoon in the month of August.' He encouraged his

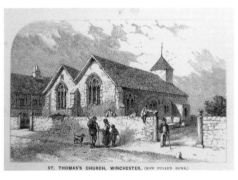

ST. THOMAS'S CHURCH, WINCHESTER, (NOW PULLED DOWN.)

Above: St Thomas' church, Winchester, which was demolished in 1845 and replaced by a new church in a nearby street

fellow preachers to divide their sermons into sections to become 'like hooks and pegs and shelves in the mind.' From 1842 he used notebooks in which to write down biblical texts and sermon divisions. 'Whenever I get hold of a text, and see my way through it, I put it down and make a note of it. If I do not see my way through a text, I cannot preach on it, because I know I cannot be simple; and if I cannot be simple,

Above: *Officers and men from the nearby Peninsular Barracks attended St Thomas' Church, Winchester when Ryle was the incumbent*

I know I had better not preach at all.' He challenged his hearers: 'Look at Christ. Seek Christ. Go to Christ.' To reach the working classes, Ryle maintained, it was essential to preach 'Christ crucified and risen again' as 'the sum and centre of our sermons, far more than we have done in the Church of England.'

Ryle believed that 'the language should be of the simplest kind ... the style should be plain, direct and conversational, with short sentences and plenty of full stops ... above all, the preacher should cultivate a lively manner. Dullness in a country pulpit is little less than a sin; and a sermon delivered in a heavy, droning, lugubrious monotone, will never be carried out of the church to the cottage or the farm.' He used proverbs and pithy sayings and spoke directly to his hearers: 'Never say "we" when you mean "I". 'In country parishes I have sometimes put before people familiar illustrations which they can see,' like a watch or a bunch of keys. He always aimed at using simple words, short sentences and memorable metaphors. Without Christ at the centre, 'your religion is a heaven without a sun, an arch without a keystone, a compass without a needle, a clock without spring or weights, a lamp without oil.' He referred to 'a stranded ship, a broken-winged eagle, a garden overrun with weeds, a harp without strings, a church in ruins.' Ryle's most frequent illustrations were about the sea, storms, ships and shipwrecks; and topically, prospecting for gold in Australia and California. On hearing Ryle preach someone remarked that sometimes his illustrations became diversions and needed to be kept in check.

As a preacher Ryle prayed for an outpouring of the Holy Spirit, for God's blessing and for a life consistent with what was said in the pulpit. But all preaching was of little use, 'unless you preach the simple gospel of Jesus Christ so fully and clearly that everybody can understand it. If Christ crucified has not his rightful place in your sermons, and sin is not exposed as it should be, and your people are not plainly told what they ought to believe, and be and do, your preaching is of no use.'

Ryle believed that it was essential to visit his parishioners. 'Sit down with your people by the fireside, and exchange thoughts with them on all subjects. Find out how they think and how they express themselves, if you want them to understand your sermons.' Amongst the poor he found an ignorance of theology and an inability to say the creed. He told the story of a country clergyman who was once asked whether he ever studied the Church Fathers of the early church. He replied that

he had little opportunity to study the *fathers* (for they were working in the fields), but he studied the *mothers* (since they were at home and he could talk to them). Ryle was critical of those well-meaning clergy who put on 'village concerts, penny readings and questionable amusements, and neglecting old-fashioned house-to-house visitation ... nothing, we may depend upon it, next to preaching the Word of God, will ever do much good to souls as quiet, friendly, face-to-face dealing with individuals.' He repeated the old adage that 'a house-going minister is one secret of a church-going people.' In his parishes Ryle made visiting a priority and later as a bishop he expected his clergy to do the same.

Above and left: *The pulpit in the new St Katherine's church, Exbury, was presented by the Ryle family with their father's favourite preaching text inscribed on it (see page 77)*

TRAVEL INFORMATION

The New Forest and surrounding area

New Forest Centre, Lyndhurst SO43 7NY
www.office@newforestmuseum.ork.uk
℃ 023 8028 4444
New Forest National Park Authority, South
Efford House, Milford Road, Lymington
SO41 0DJ
www.newforestnpa.gov.uk
℃ 01590 646600
The New Forest is the largest unenclosed
area in the south of England, and contains
a mixture of woodland, farmland, heaths,
bogs, streams and estuaries. 'Commoners'
may exercise ancient grazing rights to
permit them to allow their animals to
freely roam in the Forest. There are a
number of places to visit including nature
reserves and gardens as well as walking
the many footpaths and bridleways.

roundabout on the A326. Then follow the
brown signs for Beaulieu. The church of
St Katherine is situated in the village of
Exbury. None of the present building is
directly associated with Ryle, though the
pulpit was the gift of his family.

Exbury Gardens consists of 200 acres
on the east bank of the Beaulieu River.
The extensive gardens and narrow
gauge railway are open from March to
November, from 10.00am to 5.00pm
(but there is no public access to the
house). There are a number of exhibitions
and events, and there is good parking,
disabled access, restaurant and tea
rooms, gift shop and plant centre and an
opportunity to picnic.

Exbury Gardens

*Above: Exbury is best known today
for the stunning display of azaleas in
the Exbury Gardens*

The Estate Office, Exbury, Southampton
SO45 1AZ
www.exbury.co.uk
℃ 023 8089 1203
    To find Exbury, leave the M27 at
junction 2 and go to Dibden Purlieu

Lepe Country Park

Above: Lepe Country Park

Lepe Country Park, Exbury, Southampton
SO45 1AD
www.hants.gov.uk/lepe
℃ 023 8089 9108
    Lepe is a popular coastal country park
open throughout the year. With children's
play area, walking routes, events and café.
Free but there is a car parking charge.

MAP OF EXBURY

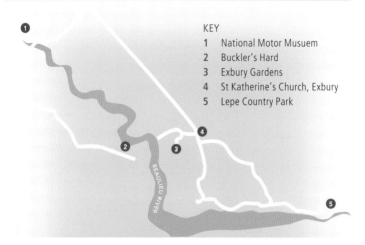

KEY

1 National Motor Musuem
2 Buckler's Hard
3 Exbury Gardens
4 St Katherine's Church, Exbury
5 Lepe Country Park

National Motor Museum

Above: *National Motor Museum, Beaulieu, Hampshire*
Beaulieu Enterprises Ltd, Beaulieu, Brockenhurst, Hampshire SO42 7ZN
www.beaulieu.co.uk
℃ 01590 612 123

Follow the signs from the village of Exbury to Beaulieu and Buckler's Hard. On the west bank of the Beaulieu River is the village of Beaulieu, where the National Motor Museum is located with its collection of 200 historic motor vehicles with numerous exhibitions, gardens, Palace House, monorail, restaurant and activities. Apart from Christmas Day it is open every day of the year from 10.00am and to 5.00pm October to May, and to 6.00pm May to September. There is free parking and disabled access.

Buckler's Hard

Beaulieu, Brockenhurst, Hampshire SO42 7XB
www.bucklershard.co.uk
℃ 01590 616 203
Follow the signs from Beaulieu to Buckler's Hard. The maritime museum depicts the prosperous shipbuilding industry here in the 18th and 19th centuries. There is also a woodland walk, café and gift shop. Apart from Christmas Day it is open from 10.00am to 4.30pm November to February; to 5.00pm March to June and September to October; to 5.30pm July and August.
Below: *Buckler's Hard, Hampshire*

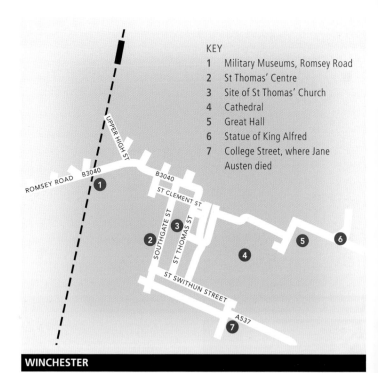

KEY

1 Military Museums, Romsey Road
2 St Thomas' Centre
3 Site of St Thomas' Church
4 Cathedral
5 Great Hall
6 Statue of King Alfred
7 College Street, where Jane Austen died

WINCHESTER

The historic city of Winchester has been an important centre since Roman times. Alfred, King of Wessex, 871–899, made Winchester his capital, and later a cathedral was established there. Winchester is situated off the M3, junction 10 (from the south) and junction 9 (from the north). As well as the cathedral, there is the Great Hall (the only remains of the castle), the Pilgrim's Hall, several military museums and the house in which Jane Austen died.

Herbert Ryle, the second son of J C Ryle, was the Bishop of Winchester from 1903 to 1911.

Tourist Information Centre, Winchester Guildhall, High Street, Winchester SO23 9GH   www.visit.winchester.co.uk
✆ 01962 840 500
Winchester Cathedral, The Chapter Office, 1 The Close, Winchester DO23 9LS
www.winchester-cathedral.org.uk
01962 857 200

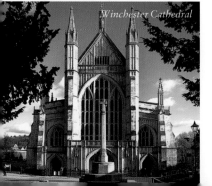

Winchester Cathedral

St Thomas' Church

St Thomas' church, where Ryle had been the incumbent, was situated in St Thomas' Street. It was demolished in 1845 and replaced by a new church in nearby Southgate Street. It was made redundant in 1970 and two years later became the Hampshire Record Office, and is now the St Thomas' Centre.

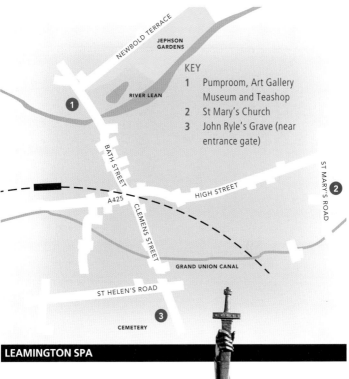

KEY

1 Pumproom, Art Gallery Museum and Teashop
2 St Mary's Church
3 John Ryle's Grave (near entrance gate)

LEAMINGTON SPA

Above: Jane Austen's house, College Street, Winchester, where she died in July 1817, aged forty-one

Right: Alfred the Great was the king of Wessex from 871. He was a man of great learning and considered to be a model Christian king

❹ 'My little parish of three hundred parishioners'

J C Ryle's small Suffolk parish was dominated by the all-powerful John Tollemache. Ryle was twice married at Helmingham, and after Matilda and Jessie died he became a single parent responsible for five young children. While he was the rector of Helmingham Ryle wrote about eighty of his tracts

In February 1844 Ryle became the rector of St Mary, Helmingham, nine miles north of Ipswich, where he remained until 1861. The area was an isolated rural community and the main crops were wheat, barley and beans. There is no village as such, and the parish consists mostly of the Helmingham estate. In 1841 there were forty-eight houses and a population of 284; twenty years later there were sixty-two houses and a population of 320. Apart from John Tollemache and the rector there were no professional people living in the locality—the rest were tenant farmers, agricultural labourers and domestic servants.

Helmingham Hall and the parish church

The rectory was adjacent to the extensive deer park around Helmingham Hall. When Ryle arrived, the rectory needed to be improved, and he stayed at the Hall while the work took place. The Tollemache family frequently entertained the great and the good and often eighteen to twenty people sat down for an evening meal. Each morning and evening Ryle led prayers for the household and Sunday was strictly observed at the Hall. Given Ryle's own social background he would have been quite at home with the Tollemache family and their numerous visitors, and the contacts he made were to become invaluable to him.

Since the Norman Conquest generations of the Tollemache family have lived in Suffolk, and they moved to Helmingham in the late 15th century. In 1829 John Tollemache inherited the Hall from his aunt and carried out an extensive restoration programme. From 1841 he was the MP for South Cheshire, then from 1868 for West Cheshire, and in 1876 he was created Baron Tollemache of Helmingham. Though politically he was a liberal-conservative, he was known as 'the labourer's Lord'. Yet Ryle observed that his parishioners 'were not interesting, living in fact in a state of servile subjection to Mr Tollemache.'

In August 1826 John Tollemache married his first

Facing page: A studio portrait of J C Ryle aged about forty

Left: A pair of the distinctive Helmingham estate cottages originally cost £300. Each Sunday every tenant was expected to attend a place of worship

cousin Georgina Louisa Best and they became the parents of eleven children, only two of whom survived infancy. Both John and Georgina were evangelical Christians and it was Georgina who was particularly supportive of Ryle's ministry. He said of her that 'her piety and devotion seemed to be the outstanding side of her character. She was an exemplary wife and mother.' Following a brief illness she died at Leamington Spa in July 1846 having gone there to be treated by Dr Henry Jephson. Her death was sudden and unexpected and Ryle believed that it affected John Tollemache's attitude towards religion in general and towards himself in particular. In January 1850 Tollemache married again and he and his wife Eliza Georgina became the parents of nine children.

Today the interior of Helmingham church is much as it was when Ryle was the incumbent. John Tollemache restored the building in 1845, and it was probably then that the numerous biblical texts were painted on the walls. Ryle's parting gift to the church was the communion table. The unusual dormer window was constructed in order to accommodate one of the monuments, many of which are to members of the Tollemache family, some fifty of whom were interred in the family vault. In 1821 the eight bells in the tower were given by Wilbraham Tollemache, and seventy years after Ryle began his ministry at Helmingham Ryle's son, Bishop Herbert Ryle, dedicated a new organ in April 1914.

Above: John Tollemache and Georgina Tollemache. John became Lord Tollemache in 1876. Ryle caustically remarked that 'the Tollemache's were very good lovers and very good haters'

'My little parish of three hundred parishioners'

When Ryle went to Helmingham, there was a small dame school in the lodge of Helmingham Hall and supervised by Georgina Tollemache, but there were issues over the new two-tier village school provided by her husband and opened in April 1854. It consisted of an upper school (for farmers' sons) and a lower school (for labourers' children). At first the local farmers were not prepared to support the venture until Tollemache sent some of own his sons to the upper school. But Ryle and his successors were not permitted to teach the church catechism to the pupils, and the situation was only resolved in 1891 when the then rector, Edward Backhouse, built a schoolroom near to the rectory and in which the catechism could be freely taught.

Ryle described his life at Helmingham. 'I have but 300 people in my parish, and have everything calculated to make the work of spiritual superintendence smooth. I have not a public house in my parish; we have not a beer-shop in the parish; there is but one place of worship, and, with the exception of about a quarter of an acre, all the parish is the property of one man, who is a sincere member of the Church of England … [yet] … I find in the spiritual cure of the 300 souls committed to my charge, not perhaps, sufficient, but, certainly, much work to be done; sin, I find, is always rife among them, and with all the preaching and all the care I can bestow, many still, I am sorry to say, remain unconverted; and, notwithstanding all the appliances of tracts, preaching and teaching, many yet remain without God and without Christ.'

In addition to conducting two Sunday services, leading a weekly prayer meeting, officiating at weddings and funerals, Ryle was

Above and Inset: *St Mary's church, Helmingham. The brass plate on the communion table in St Mary's church*

Above: *The former Helmingham rectory once occupied by Ryle and his family is now a private house. A later rector described the house as being 'dark and gloomy' and with a very small garden*

Above: *Helmingham school was opened in April 1854*

out and about throughout Suffolk, preaching in other churches and speaking at meetings in the towns and villages. He spent some time in his study—reading and writing and adding to his large library. Over the years this became a substantial collection and after his death he left most of his books to the diocese of Liverpool. During his seventeen years at Helmingham, he composed about eighty tracts, most of which were reprinted in the first seven volumes of *Home Truths* and later many appeared as chapters in his books; he also gathered collections of hymns and wrote devotional commentaries on Matthew, Mark and Luke.

The Religious Census
On 30 March 1851, the year of the Great Exhibition, a national Religious Census was conducted in the churches and chapels throughout England and Wales. It showed that out of a population of nearly eighteen million, only some 7,261,032 people had actually attended a

place of worship and of these only 52% had attended the Church of England. Every clergyman or minister was expected to complete a questionnaire and on his Census return Ryle recorded that St Mary's church could accommodate 150 people (of whom 100 people had to pay for their seats and the rest were free). On 30 March there was a morning congregation of 96 adults and an afternoon congregation of 145 adults, and a Sunday school of 27 children. Over the previous twelve months the average congregation had been 130 adults in the morning

Above: *The former Helmingham Sunday school*

Left: A studio portrait of J C Ryle aged about forty. 'We look upon him as one of the leaders of a great party in the Church' (Archdeacon William Emery)

and 200 adults in the afternoon, together with a Sunday school of 40 children. Ryle noted that 'many sit on benches in the aisles' and there was a larger congregation in the summer than in the winter. He recorded too that his income was made up of £540 from tithes, £45 from glebe-land, and £2 from fees for conducting weddings and funerals.

Ryle the preacher and pastor

What was Ryle like when he preached? Shortly before he left Helmingham a visitor recorded his impressions: 'Mr Ryle is an orator, a rhetorician, rather than a reasoner … he is an able rhetorician, and has a wonderful power of illustration, with these he works his way most successfully.' He preached without notes, and his was one of the longest sermons heard by the 'mystery churchgoer' who recorded in the *Suffolk Pulpit* that 'few, we believe, could hear such a sermon, so marked by unmistakable earnestness of purpose; so copiously and so simply illustrated, without wishing

for it a more extensive audience.'

While Ryle was a dedicated man of God he was also somewhat aloof. He confessed that 'I soon got the reputation, which I never lost, of being unsociable, distant, reserved and indisposed to encourage friendship, and not at home anywhere except in the pulpit or on the platform.' Yet he was not without evangelical friends. It was his conviction that clergy should be set apart from secular matters and he criticised those who spoke at agricultural meetings and won 'prizes for fat pigs, enormous bullocks, and large crops of turnips.' He was not prepared to make 'morning calls of courtesy and dining out, as others do.' However this sort of behaviour did not endear him to other people, but it has to be said that his reserve was also because he was a single, eligible bachelor. His standard was high, and he looked for 'a woman who was a real Christian, who was a real lady, and who was not a fool.'

Ryle's first marriage

J C Ryle married three times and his first two wives died young. In October 1845 he married Matilda Charlotte Louisa Plumptre. He was twenty-eight and she was twenty-two. Matilda was the youngest of the three daughters of John Plumptre MP of Fredville, Nonington in East Kent.

SITE OF
FORMER SUSPENSION BRIDGE
NORTH QUAY

A Suspension Bridge was opened over the River Bure
near this point on 25.4.1829.

On 2.5.1845 it collapsed with loss of 79 lives
(mostly children)

Great Yarmouth and District
Archaeology Society

Above: The terrible bridge disaster at Great Yarmouth. The bridge, which was opened in 1832, widened in 1844 and collapsed in 1845

Inset: Today the site of the bridge is marked by a blue plaque

Disaster at Great Yarmouth

On 2 May 1845 a terrible disaster took place at Great Yarmouth. The circus was in town and to publicise the event a clown was to be pulled in a wash-tub drawn by four geese on the River Bure. Thousands of people came to watch, most of whom lined the river bank while others stood or sat on the suspension bridge. As the wash-tub glided towards the bridge, hundreds rushed onto it but the sudden movement caused the bridge to collapse throwing 300 to 600 people into the river. Most of the victims were quickly rescued, but about eighty men, women and mostly children and teenagers were drowned. This 'dreadful accident' which was caused by the snapping of the suspension chains due to excess weight on the bridge, was widely reported at the time in the local and national press.

The local vicar maintained that the tragedy was the consequence of the town's sins, and several tracts were published on the disaster. One anonymous tract by 'a spiritual watchman' was called 'A word in season about the awful accident at Yarmouth'. In it Ryle challenged his readers to consider where they would be now if they had died in the accident: 'It is a fearful thing to die unprepared to meet God. What is your own life? Are you living unto God? Are you a true Christian? Have you really repented of your sins and turned from them? Have you actually come unto Christ and believed on him for salvation?' He urged his readers to 'consider your own ways' and 'be reconciled to God'.

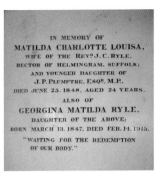

IN MEMORY OF
MATILDA CHARLOTTE LOUISA,
WIFE OF THE REVᴰ J.C. RYLE.
RECTOR OF HELMINGHAM, SUFFOLK:
AND YOUNGER DAUGHTER OF
J.P. PLUMPTRE, ESQᴿ. M.P.
DIED JUNE 25. 1848, AGED 24 YEARS.
ALSO OF
GEORGINA MATILDA RYLE,
DAUGHTER OF THE ABOVE:
BORN MARCH 13. 1847, DIED FEB. 14. 1915.
"WAITING FOR THE REDEMPTION
OF OUR BODY."

Above: Memorial tablet to Matilda Ryle in St Mary the Virgin, Nonington (on the wall behind the organ)

Following the premature birth of Georgina Matilda in March 1847, her mother developed a rare form of postnatal depression in which she suffered from delusions and other psychotic symptoms. John Plumptre provided a house for them in Tunbridge Wells, and every three weeks Ryle visited his wife and child. By September they all returned to Helmingham, but then Matilda developed consumption and for several months the family with their two servants stayed at Ventnor on the Isle of Wight. In February 1848 John and Catherine Plumptre remained with them until in May they went to stay with Ryle's parents at Anglesey, then to Tunbridge Wells and finally to Fredville, where Matilda died in June, and her body was interred in the family vault in Nonington church. In August the heart-broken Ryle went to Scotland with his father-on-law, John Plumptre, and his brother-in-law, Algernon Coote. At first Ryle's daughter Georgina lived with her grandparents at Fredville and once a month Ryle made the long journey from Helmingham to visit her. Nothing is known about her adult life, apart from the fact that she died in Roehampton and was also interred at Nonington.

Ryle's second marriage

In February 1850 Ryle married Jessie Elizabeth Walker. She was the eldest daughter of John Walker, a London merchant with an estate at Crawfordton, near Monaire, Dumfries and Galloway, Scotland. Jessie was already known to the Ryle family, and was a godparent of Georgina. On her marriage, Jessie became the step-mother to Georgina and the mother of five children of her own—Jessie Isabelle, an unnamed prematurely-born daughter who died about an hour after her birth, Reginald John, Herbert Edward and Arthur Johnston. Isabelle, who was 'tall and dark, with a fresh complexion' remained unmarried and died in November 1921.

Above: The interior of St Mary's church, Helmingham

John Pemberton Plumptre (1791–1864)

John Plumptre of Fredville, Nonington, Kent, was a serious and sober evangelical who was active in local and national affairs and a generous benefactor. His memorial in Nonington church records that he was 'a confessor of Christ before men'. He was a barrister in Lincoln's Inn for three years before becoming a partner in the Canterbury Bank—one of the largest and best managed private banks in Kent. In 1918 it became part of Lloyds Bank. From 1832 to 1852 Plumptre was the MP for

Inset: *John and Matilda Plumptre of Fredville, Nonington*

East Kent. Politically he was a conservative and his Christian convictions were evident in his strong support for Sunday observance. At the same time he was a commissioner of the Dover Harbour Board, and from 1858 to 1861 a deputy Lord Warden of the

Cinque Ports and Lieutenant Governor of Dover Castle.

In his younger days John Plumptre became fond of Fanny, the niece of Jane Austen. She was a frequent visitor to her brother

Edward at Godmersham Park, near Chilham (possibly the inspiration for 'Pemberley' in *Pride and Prejudice*). Having met Plumptre, Jane described him as 'a handsome young man certainly with quiet, gentlemanlike manners. I set him down as sensible rather than brilliant'. However nothing came of the relationship and in April 1818 Plumptre married Catherine Matilda Methuen. They had a family of three daughters, the first (Catherine Emma) died young, the second (Cecilia Matilda) married Ryle's long-standing friend Algernon Coote (who became the vicar of Nonington) and the third (Matilda Charlotte Louisa) who married J C Ryle.

Throughout her married life Jessie Ryle suffered from poor health and she and her husband often stayed in London while she had medical treatment or gave birth to their children. They stayed first in Onslow Square, and then rented a house in Onslow Crescent, and subsequently in St Leonard's Terrace, Chelsea. These periods away from Helmingham were significant for Ryle, and he 'became acquainted with all the leading evangelical clergy and laity in London, and was brought forward continually as a speaker and preacher in every part of the metropolis.'

After ten years of marriage Jessie was diagnosed with Bright's disease and died soon afterwards in May 1860. Her death Ryle described as a 'heavy domestic affliction.' Sadly Herbert Ryle's only childhood recollection of Helmingham rectory was being held up by his nurse, Mary Parker, and looking out of an upper window to watch his mother's funeral procession pass from the house to the church. Jessie was interred in the churchyard on the north side of the church and out of sight of the rectory windows. There is an apocryphal story about a visitor to the church who enquired where Ryle's wife was buried: 'He usually buries them at Helmingham' the parish clerk replied dryly! After Jessie's death her unmarried sisters Eliza and Caroline helped to look after the five surviving children then aged between three and thirteen years.

Ryle's *Autobiography* ended with the death of Jessie. For the past five years he had experienced 'much wear and tear and anxiety of mind and body … As to holidays, rest and relaxation in the year, I never had any at all; while the whole business of entertaining and amusing three little boys in an evening devolved entirely upon me. In fact the whole state of things was a heavy strain upon me, both in body and mind, and I often wonder how I lived through it.' However, he learnt something about being a parent, and remarked that 'the minister, who has no sons and daughters of his own, suffers immense loss in the study of human nature.'

Three generations

Reginald John Ryle (1854–1922) who was educated at Hill House, Wadhurst, Sussex, then Repton, and after graduating from Trinity College, Cambridge became a medical doctor. In time he became a rationalist and a friend of the Huxley family. He married Catherine Scott and of their ten children, John Alfred Ryle (1889–1950) became an eminent London physician. In 1935 he was appointed the regus Professor of Physic at Cambridge and in 1943, the first Professor of the Institute of Social Medicine at Oxford. He was a humanist,

and like his father, a pacifist; and Gilbert (1900–1976) who had a twin sister Mary, became a distinguished lecturer in philosophy at Oxford, and in 1945 the Waynflete Professor of metaphysical philosophy. Sir Martin Ryle (1918–1984) the second son of John Alfred Ryle (and great-grandson of J C Ryle), became Professor of Radio Astronomy at Cambridge

Above: The three Plumptre sisters— Catherine, Cecilia and Matilda

in 1959, the Astronomer Royal in 1972 and two years later shared the Nobel Prize for physics. He was knighted in 1966.

Herbert Edward Ryle (1856–1925) was also educated at Wadhurst, then Eton College and graduated from King's College, Cambridge. He pursued an academic career and became the Hulsean Professor of Divinity at Cambridge and President of Queens' College, and after being ordained married Nea Adams. From 1883 to 1887 he

Below: Jessie Ryle's gravestone is in the graveyard on the north side of Helmingham church

was an examining chaplain to his father, and although they were close, Herbert steadily adopted a more liberal attitude towards the Old Testament. In 1901 he became the Bishop of Exeter and was translated to Winchester in 1903 and from 1911 he was the Dean of Westminster. His ministry at the Abbey is commemorated by the nearby 'Dean Ryle Street'.

Arthur Johnston Ryle (1857–1915) was also educated at Wadhurst, then Eton College and graduated from New College, Oxford. He had wanted to study art in Paris, but was advised against it by his father who warned him about the 'moral dangers' of the city. Arthur, who remained unmarried, pursued his artistic career had a studio in Thurlow Square, London and was a member of the Royal Society of British Artists. He was a passionate golfer and had a holiday house near the fairway of the Royal Dornoch golf course in Scotland. To mark his love of the game the Ryle Memorial Medal was presented to The Professional Golfers Association and is now awarded to the winner of the Open Championship if the champion is a member of the Association.

Arthur Ryle died in 1915 of 'cerebral meningitis' while he worked in the YMCA in Felixstowe, Suffolk.

Money matters

Ryle never fully recovered from the loss of his family fortune. He felt disgraced that he had come down in the world and was forced to live on what he considered to be an inadequate income. Years later he even complained about the cost of medical treatment for his first wife: 'Again, as on fifty other occasions, I found

Above: The Ryle Memorial Medal in memory of Arthur Ryle is annually awarded to the winner of the golf Open Championship

the misery of being a poor man.' But by contemporary standards he was not impoverished. Certainly he had been a poor curate in Exbury, but his income increased in Winchester, and he had an even larger stipend at Helmingham. However, even then he maintained that it was a struggle to survive on a stipend of over £500 a year, together with £200 from his wife. His complaining was unnecessary, for many of his fellow clergy had to survive on a stipend of upwards of £150 a year.

Before his first marriage, Ryle employed a cook, a housemaid and a man who looked after his garden and his horse. In the Census of 1861 the rectory household consisted of Ryle, his five young children, his two sisters-in-law, together with six servants (a housekeeper, a governess, a nurse and three maids). Over the years his income steadily increased. As the vicar of Stradbroke his annual stipend was just over £1,000 and on becoming the Bishop of Liverpool he received £4,000 a year. In the 1891 Census he had two footmen, a cook-housekeeper and seven maids. As a bishop he gave donations to many worthy causes including gifts to deserving parishes in his diocese, and when he died in June 1900 he left a small fortune of £26,662 4s 8d— worth something over a million and a half pounds in today's currency.

WANTED,

A good plain cook to act as housekeeper, in a clergyman's family, containing FIVE children and SIX servants.
Assistance given to the kitchen. Good references indispensable. Wages **£20** with tea, sugar and washing.
ADDRESS, REV. J C RYLE, Helmingham Rectory, Stonham, Suffolk.

Above: *Advert as found in the* Ipswich Journal, *22 December 1860*

Above: *Three generations of the Ryle family—J C Ryle, his son Herbert and grandson Edward*

TRAVEL INFORMATION

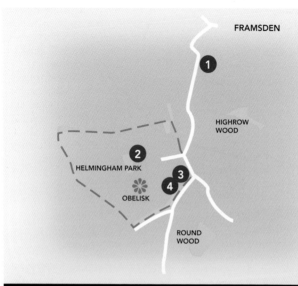

MAP OF HELMINGHAM

KEY

1 The Village School
2 Helmingham Hall

3 Old Rectory
4 St Mary's Church

Helmingham and Stradbroke

Ryle's Suffolk parishes are both east of the A140. Stradbroke is about twenty-five miles south of Norwich. The village is off the A140 on the B1117. After going through Eye, Stradbroke is at the junction of the B1117 and B1118. All Saints' church is in the centre of the village.

Helmingham is about ten miles south of Stradbroke. At the junction of the A140 and the A1120 follow the signs for Stonham Aspal and Pettaugh. Helmingham is to the south of the A1120 and off the B1077. St Mary's church and rectory (now a private house) are adjacent to the Helmingham Hall park.

For a visitor to the area, a useful base from which to visit Helmingham and Stradbroke is the attractive market town of Framlingham, situated off the A1120 on the B1116. There are a number of places to stay and also places in which to eat. English Heritage is responsible for the 12th century Castle, from which can be seen The Mere (known for its wildlife) and the town. Nearby is the Second World War Airfield (in use from 1943 to 1949) with a small museum.

Above: *Helmingham Hall gardens*

Helmingham Hall Gardens

The Events Office, Helmingham, Stowmarket, Suffolk 1P14 6EF
www.helmingham.com
℅ 01473 890 799

Helmingham Hall is the private residence of Lord and Lady Tollemache and the gardens are well worth a visit. While some of the gardens date from the 18th century, many have been created during the past forty years. The park consists of about 400 acres and contains both red and fallow deer; some of the oak trees are reputed to be 900 years old, and the avenue of trees leading to the Hall was planted in the 1680s. Helmingham Hall is surrounded by a moat and each evening the two drawbridges are raised.

The house is not open to the public. There is a car park, gift shop, and tea rooms, with disabled access to the gardens which are open from May to September, on Sunday, Tuesday, Wednesday, Thursday, 12.00noon to 5.00pm.

British Bird of Prey Centre

Stonham Barns, Pettaugh Road, Stonham Aspal, Suffolk 1P14 6AT
www.falconry-east.co.uk
℅ 01449 711425

The Centre, which holds a variety of activity days and falconry courses, also includes the Suffolk Owl Sanctuary, a garden centre, gift and craft shops, golf course and places in which to eat. Open daily 10.00am to 7.00pm.

Teapot Pottery

Carter's Teapot Pottery, Low Road, Debenham, Suffolk 1P14 6QU
www.cartersteapots.com
℅ 01728 860 475

Teapot manufacture, shop and tea-shop.

The Teapot Pottery is in Low Road, off High Street, Debenham, and is situated off the B1077. Open Monday to Friday 9.00am to 5.30pm; Saturday 10.30am to 4.30pm; Sunday 2.00pm to 5.00pm.

⑤ An ever expanding ministry

Soon after J C Ryle moved to Stradbroke he married again. He had a larger parish, an increased income, and curates to assist him with his parochial duties. Ryle continued to write tracts and also became a well-known national speaker

In September 1861 Ryle became the vicar of All Saints, Stradbroke, ten miles north of Helmingham, and lived there until he became the first Bishop of Liverpool in 1880. Though the parish was poor, his income was just over £1,000 a year, and there being no resident landlords, he was probably the wealthiest man in the village. Ryle was appointed to one of the most prestigious livings in the diocese by John Pelham, the evangelical Bishop of Norwich. Before the 20th century the parishes of Helmingham and Stradbroke were part of that diocese and were transferred to the newly-created diocese of St Edmundsbury in 1914.

Stradbroke and a third marriage

Stradbroke is an extensive parish of 3,702 acres, and includes a number of isolated hamlets as well as the village. In Ryle's day the nearest railway stations were nine miles away at Diss and seven miles at Harleston, and he often left it to the last minute to get to the station. 'Garnham, we shall lose the train', he would call out to the coachman through the carriage window. This command was invariably met with the response: 'I can't go faster, sir, unless the horses gallop.' 'Then make them gallop' would be the reply—and through the main street of Harleston the horses would dash at a pace that brought people running to their doors to see 'old Ryle late again.' While he lived in Suffolk Ryle made frequent use of the railways and travelled long distances to speak in about twenty cities throughout England, Wales and Ireland.

In 1861 Stradbroke had a population of 1,537 but by 1881

Above: *All Saints' church, Stradbroke, was restored in two stages in 1872 and 1879*

Facing page: *The Stradbroke village sign, standing near the site of the old vicarage, is of Bishop Robert Grosseteste*

Above: *The village street, Stradbroke. A photograph from the 1860s by Henrietta Ryle*

it had declined to 1,202 and throughout those twenty years there were about 300 inhabited houses. Ryle described 400 of his parishioners as 'farmers, tradesmen and professional persons' but the majority were impoverished agricultural labourers. During the bad winter of 1878–79 forty parishioners received free coal. One way to escape from dire poverty was to emigrate to the then colonies. The decrease in population

Below: *Stradbroke Workhouse closed in 1871*

Above: *Broughton Old Hall, Salford, the home of the Clowes family*

also came about by people moving from the country to find employment in the industrial towns of the north and by the closure of the workhouse in 1871, whose inmates were officially described as 'paupers, patients and lunatics'.

Like other rural communities, Stradbroke was reasonably self-sufficient. Twice a month there was a corn market, and during the spring and summer a weekly livestock market. There were butchers, grocers, and tradesmen such as boot and shoe makers, tailors, milliners, joiners, blacksmiths, saddlers and watchmakers. There was also a police station with two resident policemen. Apart from the parish church, the only other place of worship was a Baptist Chapel. Ryle calculated that one third of the parish had a Baptist background and the rest would describe themselves as Church of England although, he observed, the labourers knew 'little of any distinction in religion.' But with their vicar's clear biblical teaching few parishioners would have failed to grasp what the Christian faith was about.

Ryle arrived at Stradbroke as a widower and in October 1861 he married his third wife who became the step-mother to his five children. Henrietta Amelia Clowes was a daughter of Colonel William and Antonia Clowes of Broughton Old Hall, Salford, Lancashire. Henrietta was a distant relative of Ryle's mother and he had known her for some time. She was an accomplished organist and talented photographer, and some of her work may be seen today in Stradbroke church.

The vicarage, in which the Ryle family lived together with their servants, was enlarged and repaired in 1863, demolished in

Right: *Stradbroke vicarage was the home of the Ryle family. The house was occupied by the incumbents of Stradbroke until 1947 when it was sold and privately occupied until it was demolished for housing development in the 1960s*

STRADBROKE VICARAGE, SUFFOLK.

the 1960s, and all that remains today is part of the garden wall. A young visitor to the vicarage described what he found: 'Mr Ryle, with his gigantic figure and stentorian voice, was perhaps rather formidable to a youthful visitor, but he was very kind and hearty, and I soon felt at home. The boys, each in his way, were delightful companions. The atmosphere of the house was like that of my own home, devotional daily Bible readings, somewhat lengthy family prayers, and a good deal of religious talk. But all was quite wholesome and unpretentious, and I don't think any of us were bored, much less inclined to cavil at the regime, at any rate at the time.'

They were a close-knit family and Ryle thoroughly approved of family gatherings at Christmas. Yet he was also serious and sober and against 'foolish talking, and jesting, and joking, and excessive merriment' and he disapproved of popular publications like *Punch* and *Pickwick*.

Herbert Ryle recalled his childhood and had fond memories of his 'dear old father':

'In the country life of Suffolk he was everything to us, taught us games, natural history, astronomy, and insisted on our never being idle, and carefully fostered our love of books.' The three brothers, who apparently never quarrelled, were very close to each other, learnt carpentry and had their work bench in their father's study. 'To us boys he was extraordinarily indulgent. And he was tolerant to a degree little known or recognised … since the time I went to school at the age of nine and a half I never received from him a harsh word. And the sense of companionship grew between us until the rarity of meeting one another caused that growth to cease, and simply left us supremely happy to meet and be together.'

During almost twenty years at Stradbroke Ryle completed his commentaries on the four gospels and composed about 120 tracts, many of which were subsequently republished as chapters in his books. In addition he wrote a number of historical biographies and made proposals for church reform. All of this took place

---

Robert Grosseteste (1175–1253)

Apart from Ryle, the most famous son of Stradbroke was Robert Grosseteste. He was born in the parish and came from a humble family. After studying at Oxford and Paris, he held high office at the University of Oxford where he actively supported the Franciscans after they had arrived in the city. In 1235 Grosseteste became the Bishop of Lincoln and though a strong supporter of the papacy, he was critical of unsuitable and unqualified Italians holding clerical positions in England and whom he considered to be 'the poison of the serpent'.

As a bishop he was diligent and responsible, and his relationship with the monarch was cool and critical.

Grosseteste was an extraordinarily able scholar, for as well as fulfilling his spiritual responsibilities he was well-known for his learning as a lawyer, philosopher, natural scientist, physicist, poet, agriculturalist and theologian. He composed a large number of commentaries, translations and sermons, and for two hundred years was regarded as a man of great learning. After his death in October 1253 he was interred in the south transept of Lincoln cathedral. In Lincoln his name is associated with the Bishop Grosseteste University College, which originated as a training college for women teachers in 1862 and gained University College status in 2006.

Above: The monument to Bishop Robert Grosseteste is in the south transept of Lincoln Cathedral

---

alongside his increasingly important national role and his personal circumstances which he listed as 'deaths, domestic anxieties [and] illness' as well as moving house. These deaths would have included his daughter, his second wife, his father and father-in-law. There were also the demands of his larger parish: 'What endless petty interruptions a clergyman must submit to in a poor rural parish of 1,400 people, where there is no resident landlord, and no layman who has leisure, and where many things must necessarily hinge on the clergyman, no one can know unless he has filled the position.'

Shared ministry and revival

In Stradbroke Ryle had a succession of curates to assist him in his work: Adam Washington, followed by his younger brother Robert, then John Toolis, Clement Sneyd and Edward Stead. For a few months in 1865 Charles Mules assisted in the parish. He then resumed his curacy in County Durham, moved to New Zealand in 1868, and from 1892 to 1912 was the Bishop of Nelson. It was these assistant clergy who conducted the majority of the baptisms, weddings and funerals, and officiated when Ryle was absent from the parish. However he

Above: The Stradbroke schools were opened in January 1864. A photograph from the 1860s by Henrietta Ryle

did conduct a number of these 'occasional offices' and on one day in June 1869 he baptised one adult and ten children!

Ryle made full use of lay members of the congregation: 'My principle is [to] do nothing without the laity.' Like other evangelical parishes at the time, Stradbroke had a team of district visitors who visited the poor, read the Bible to them and distributed copies of Ryle's latest tracts. During the summer months open air meetings were held in the village, and in the winter evenings in homes throughout the parish. The Sunday school, which had a number of teachers including members of the Ryle family, met in the church school. Ryle gave his support to the Temperance Movement, to the 10th Suffolk Rifle Volunteer Corps, to the local cricket team and provided a reading room as an alternative to the two inns and four beer houses.

In one of his tracts Ryle observed that 'a lunatic asylum is a pitiable sight', and later he was moved by the plight of Edward Boon and paid for his clothes and gave £125 for his care in the Eastern Counties Asylum for Idiots and Imbeciles in Colchester. After five years Boon was transferred to the Royal Albert Asylum, Lancashire where, it may be assumed, Ryle continued to support him.

Inset: *The same Stradbroke school today*

In 1859 the second evangelical awakening took place and the revival that had began in America, spread throughout the United Kingdom. While some evangelicals were critical of what was happening, Ryle set out his views in an address he gave to the Islington Clerical Meeting on 'How can a revival of spiritual religion be promoted among the clergy?' Revival meetings were held throughout Suffolk and when the evangelists Reginald Radcliffe and Shuldham Henry were in the county early in 1861 they preached in a number of churches and chapels, and on visiting Ipswich Ryle acted as their sponsor. When the two evangelists spoke in Lowestoft large numbers of people flocked to hear them, and within a matter of weeks there were 500 converts.

The church schools

Before 1864 only a few children in Stradbroke received a minimal education. There was a parish school for about twenty boys conducted by a 77 year old master in a dilapidated timber building, and with a temporary school for about thirty-five girls in a room hired by Ryle. However, once the new schools were open, the master was pensioned off and the two schools closed.

Already at Helmingham there was an upper school and a lower school and this same principle was adopted at Stradbroke. The upper school was for about 40 to 50 sons of farmers and tradesmen and the annual fees were £100. About half of these pupils came from the parish of Stradbroke and the rest from neighbouring parishes. The pupils walked or rode ponies

or donkeys and, if necessary, could lodge in the village. Each year about three boys went onto Framlingham College. The lower school, of between 230 to 250 pupils none of whom were more than ten years old, was for the sons and daughters of labourers.

The headmaster taught the upper school and superintended both schools, and the lower school also had a headmistress. In addition there was an under master and two pupil teachers. A connecting door, through which the headmaster alone could pass, joined the two schools, and separate entrances, toilets and playgrounds for the two schools. This division was partly social and partly financial, and the fees from the upper school helped to subsidize the running of both schools. The running costs of about £300 a year were from a government grant, a small endowment, one penny a week from the lower school pupils, voluntary contributions and about £30 a year from Ryle. The buildings and land cost about £1,300 and the schools were opened in January 1864 after a service in the parish church at

which the preacher was the Bishop of Rochester. Later in the year Henrietta Ryle was there with her camera , and her photograph shows her tall husband soberly dressed in a black suit and tall top hat, standing in front of the new building and towering over the small children in the playground.

The parish church

In 1823 All Saints' church had been repaired and re-pewed and in 1835 an organ had been purchased for £150. Large box pews replaced the earlier seating and pew rents were paid by 407 people. In addition there were another 221 free seats for the poor in the aisles, and free seating for 112 boys and girls near the font. There were further seats for thirteen singers in the west gallery, making a total capacity of 753 seats.

Ryle initiated a thorough restoration of the building and it took place in two stages, in 1871–72 and in 1879. In all a sum of £5,000 was required and since it was beyond the resources of the parish, he published appeals for the funds. The amount required was received from voluntary contributions (donations of under

£5 from over thirty parishioners), and larger amounts of £200 each from six of Ryle's friends: the banker Robert Bevan, the brewer Robert Hanbury, Robert Holden, Mrs Laurie, the philanthropist George Moore and the wealthy Suffolk clergyman Edmund Hollond. Ryle himself contributed £150, and two of his daughters gave £100 towards the purchase of a new organ and a clock for the tower. In an appeal letter Ryle outlined what needed to be done.

George Moore (1806–1876)

Above: The Christian philanthropist, George Moore

One of those who contributed £200 for the restoration of Stradbroke church was the Anglican philanthropist George Moore. He came from humble origins in Cumbria, where he served as an apprentice draper before moving to London in 1825. Though he had little formal education, he was very hard-working and soon became a partner in a firm involved in the lace trade, from which he eventually amassed a considerable fortune. His philosophy was simple: 'I feel it is God's money I have to give away.' This he freely distributed to numerous individuals, and to charitable and educational causes in London and Cumbria. His faith was equally simple: 'I have no wavering about the inspiration of the Word—no picking and choosing amid alleged myths—no paring down of the atonement.'

After his Christian conversion in the early 1850s he made donations to agencies like the London City Mission and to the County Towns' Mission. He supported clergy and lay workers, and gave away thousands of copies of the Bible, Christian tracts and books. These included gifts of Ryle's tracts to Scripture Readers and 2,500 copies of Ryle's *Expository Thoughts on the Gospels.* Inside each copy was the inscription: 'Presented to … by George Moore on condition that a portion of this book is read every day.' Moore was a humble, self-made man whose life is summed up by the text on the wall of his study: 'Charity never faileth' (1 Corinthians 13:8).

'The principal roof of the nave needs close attention. The stonework and tracery of the clerestory windows is decayed, and must be entirely renewed. The roof of both the side aisles are in such a rotten state that they must be taken off, and replaced by new roofs. The whole area of the interior needs to be re-floored and reseated. The chancel gable and south porch must be taken down and rebuilt, as well as part of the north porch. The tower needs repairs of several kinds, from top to bottom; and the magnificent tower arch is blocked up and hidden by a huge screen of lath and plaster. New doors are required throughout the building. The clock and the organ are both in a dilapidated and contemptible condition. The whole building needs to be warmed. At present it is so miserably cold in winter, that old and delicate people cannot attend the worship of God without serious risk or discomfort.'

In addition to the restoration,

Above: George Moore's monument in the south transept of Carlisle cathedral

Below: George Moore's dedication inside a copy of Ryle's Expository Thoughts on the Gospels

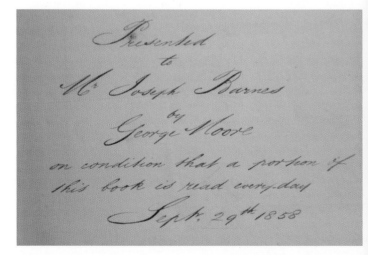

Right: The interior of All Saints' church, Stradbroke

Below: The inscription on the ledge of the pulpit showing J C Ryle's crude underlining of the word 'not' (see page 47)

two cottages on the south side of the church were demolished, improving the view of the church and making it possible to enlarge the churchyard.

Ryle also made known what was needed by appealing for funds in some of his tracts. He stated that 'before the connection of the present vicar of Stradbroke with his parish is ended, he is anxious to leave every part of his church in such complete order, that no fair excuse may be left to any succeeding vicar for introducing ornaments or fittings of an un-protestant character. He wishes, in short, to leave his church a complete pattern of what the House of God ought to be in the Reformed Church of England.' This proved to be the case and since Ryle's time very few changes have taken place, and the building remains much as he left it, apart from the removal of some pews, and as recently as 1951 when permission was granted to place candlesticks on the communion table. In 1952 two more bells were hung (making a peal of ten)—one named after Bishop Grosseteste and the other after Bishop Ryle.

The restored building was dedicated by the Bishop of Norwich on 3 April 1872, and in the following year the new organ was used for the first time. The bishop returned on 30 October 1879 and preached at the opening of the chancel restored at the cost of £700 (given by J C Ryle) in memory of his father, and in the same year two more bells were added to the original six.

For a congregation sitting in the nave, the challenge of the text above the chancel arch is clear: 'Believe on the Lord Jesus Christ, and thou shalt be saved' (Acts 16:31). Further texts are painted on the roof trusses and, other texts were painted on metal plates attached to the walls. The 17th century communion table remains

Above: *Taken by Henrietta Ryle near the school*

in the church but the pulpit from the same period was removed during the restoration. On the ledge of the new pulpit is the text 'Woe is unto me, if I preach *not* the gospel' (1 Corinthians 9:16). After the lettering had been carved, Ryle took the workman's mallet and chisel and crudely underlined the word 'not'. His action made clear his priority to continue to preach the good news to his congregation. However eight months later he was no longer the vicar of Stradbroke, but the Bishop of Liverpool. In 1891 he returned to his former parish and unveiled a commemorative plaque in the tower.

Personal circumstances

In 1869 Ryle became the rural dean of Hoxne (pronounced 'Hoxon'). A deanery is a group of adjacent Anglican parishes, and in February 1872 he was appointed an honorary canon of Norwich cathedral, making him 'Canon Ryle'. In May of the same year he was due to speak to a meeting of forty-two clergy in King's Lynn on 'the adaptation of church services to the wants of present times.' But he was unable to be present and an Anglo-Catholic critic noted that 'he sent his paper (accompanied by an off-hand note full of self-importance) for [Nicholas] Garry, the secretary, to read for him. Considering the hieroglyphics in which Mr Ryle writes, it is a wonder that the reader accomplished the task.'

In the autumn of 1874 Ryle was seriously ill and this prevented him from undertaking all speaking engagements outside his parish. When he was stronger, he and his wife visited their friend George Moore, who reported that 'our dear friends the Ryles arrived; very glad we were to receive them. Thank God he has recovered from his severe illness. He is one of the salt of the earth. May he long be spared to work for Christ!' Such expressions of support for Ryle were common among most of his fellow evangelicals, but he was severely criticised by his ritualistic opponents.

TRAVEL INFORMATION

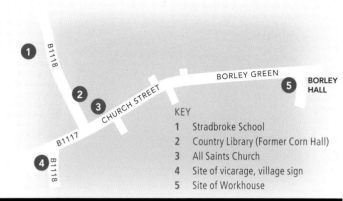

KEY

1 Stradbroke School
2 Country Library (Former Corn Hall)
3 All Saints Church
4 Site of vicarage, village sign
5 Site of Workhouse

MAP OF STRADBROKE

Left: The former Corn Hall, Stradbroke is now the County Library. Ryle often spoke in the building and as the rural dean of Hoxne chaired meetings of the deanery

Stradbroke

The village of Stradbroke is a compact community with All Saints church at the centre of the village. Nearby is the church school, the site of the vicarage, the village sign, the Baptist chapel and the County Library. For the history of the village contact the Stradbroke Local History Group www.stradbroke.org.uk

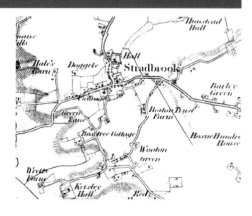

Above: A map of Stradbroke in the time of Ryle

⑥ The prince of tract writers

J C Ryle wrote about two hundred tracts, most of which were widely circulated and some were translated into about ten other languages. Later many of the tracts became chapters in his books and some of which can now be read on the Internet

After the invention of printing, political pamphlets and religious tracts became a very popular means of mass communication. Whereas today tracts consist of just a few pages, in the past they were more substantial. Millions of tracts were published in the 19th century, and cheap printing and increased literacy meant that they were widely circulated and avidly read. While some were published by bodies like the Religious Tract Society, others were written by enterprising clergy and ministers. Most of them had a limited circulation but Ryle's tracts were read throughout the world and translated into at least ten other languages. Tract distributors included the clergy, Scripture Readers and parish visitors. The philanthropist George Moore provided the Scripture Readers of Cumbria with Ryle's tracts, and some of his tracts and hymn books were distributed among the soldiers fighting in the Crimea War.

Ryle's many friends distributed his tracts. William Marsh preferred Ryle's tracts above all others and Alfred Christopher, the rector of St Aldate's, Oxford used every possible opportunity to distribute them: 'Do not simply use those directed against ritualistic or Romish errors. Give the people the gospel tracts as well. Give them, for example, that well-guarded Scripture tract on "Assurance". Then do all that you can to promote the reading in families of Mr Ryle's *Expository Thoughts on the Gospels*. If they are read,

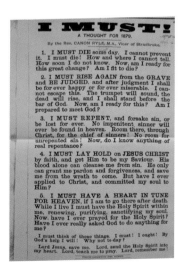

Above: *One of Ryle's cottage tracts (about A3 in size)*

Facing page: *The pulpit in St Mary's, Helmingham from which Ryle delivered his sermons*

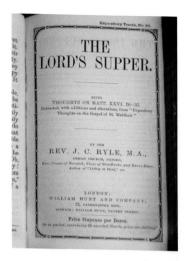

Left: For Ryle, the usual sequence was a sermon, then a tract and finally a chapter in a book

All of Ryle's tracts were a clear presentation of the evangelical faith. They were addressed to the 'Reader', and ended 'I remain your affectionate friend, J C Ryle.' They were so distinctive that his former headmaster observed that 'none but an Eton boy could write such English.' They were simple in style, mostly evangelistic in content and always challenging to the reader. They had short pithy titles like 'The cross', 'Be zealous' and 'Beware!' While some tracts were short, others like 'Assurance' and 'How readest thou?' were longer. Sometimes the longer tracts were subdivided and re-published as shorter tracts and having different titles. There was also

the Spirit of God will bless them, and they will lay hold of the hearts of many.' Christopher distributed 1,000 copies of Ryle's tract 'Are you forgiven?' to all members of the university, and each year his holiday reading included *Christian Leaders of the 18th Century*. When Christopher embarrassed members of his family by giving out tracts at garden parties they emptied his pockets, only to discover that he had taken the precaution of concealing a supply inside his elastic-sided boots!

In all, Ryle wrote about 200 tracts for adults and children and with an estimated circulation of twelve million copies. Two of the most popular tracts were 'Do you pray?' (130,000 copies published) and 'Living or Dead?' (110,000 copies published). Standing alongside Ryle as a popular communicator was William Hunt, his sympathetic printer and publisher. Hunt was an enterprising individual who provided cheap and readable tracts for the mass market.

Above: Many of the books by Ryle are still published in the UK and USA

a series of single broadsheets intended for display on cottage walls.

Ryle's smaller tracts cost 1d or 2d each, the larger ones from 4d and assorted packets were a shilling. Between 1851 and 1871 seventy-five of his tracts were published as chapters in eight volumes of *Home Truths*, and many of these tracts subsequently became the basis of his trilogy: *Knots Untied, Old Paths, Practical Religion*, and also in *Holiness*. While the tracts were intended for a popular readership, Ryle knew that many people might not read a tract but they might be 'more

William Hunt printer and publisher

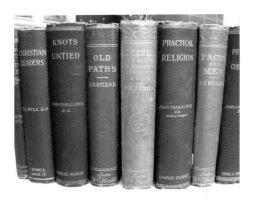

Above: Ryle wrote books on practical Christianity, theology and church history. In his day they were all hard bound

In the 1820's Edward Hunt of Tavern Street, Ipswich was a printer, bookseller and stationer who was later joined by his sons, Edward and William. In the early 1850s William bought his father's business and the publications listed in his extensive catalogue were sent post free. William Hunt was an evangelical and a member of the Ipswich branch of the Church Association, and for nearly forty years was responsible for the publication of most of Ryle's tracts and books. He also published the writings of other evangelical clergy, but none of them were as popular as Ryle. Hunt suggested that Ryle should edit an evangelical magazine, but he declined and instead proposed that he and his fellow evangelicals should publish a series of 'Ipswich Tracts'. But when nothing came of this, Ryle and Hunt worked together.

In 1864 Hunt went into partnership with William MacIntosh of London as 'William Hunt and Co', and three years later, when their partnership was dissolved, Hunt retained premises in London and Ipswich. However in May 1883 he had debts of nearly £20,000 and went bankrupt through the dishonesty of two of his clerks and from his inability to sell the remaining stock of Ryle's publications.

Ryle's next publisher, Charles J. Thynne of London, was referred to as the 'successor to William Hunt and Co', and from the late 1890s Ryle's publisher was Drummond's Tract Depot of Stirling, Scotland. Since then other publishers in the UK and USA have published Ryle's tracts and books, and many of them are available on the Internet.

Above: '*I have somewhat to say unto thee*'—Ryle's first published sermon

willing to [purchase and] read a volume.' Always Ryle wanted his tracts to be read: 'My heart's desire and prayer to God is that this subject may be greatly useful to your soul. I entreat you to give it a fair reading. Do not put it on the fire. Do not tear it in pieces. Read it! Read it! Read it to the end!' While the tracts were avidly read outside his parishes, some of his parishioners didn't always receive their copies, and were subsequently found dumped in local ditches by his young distributors.

At Helmingham Ryle published his first sermon: 'I have somewhat to say unto thee' (Luke 7:40) in which he urged his readers to be saved. He challenged them to 'read the Bible. Read it regularly. Read it all. Be a Bible-reading Christian', to 'pray without ceasing', and to 'remember the Sabbath day, to keep it holy [and] go to some place of worship where the gospel is preached.' These themes of personal faith, daily Bible reading, persistent prayer, Sunday observance and regular public worship became the staple fare of Ryle's tracts. Sometimes he responded to contemporary issues, like the cattle plague and an outbreak of cholera, but the majority of his tracts were the sermons he preached and specially written Christmas messages and New Year 'Questions' addressed to his rural parishioners.

Much of Ryle's teaching was shaped by his convictions about the second coming of Christ and a literal fulfilment of unfulfilled Old Testament prophecy: 'The time is short the Lord is at hand. A few short years and the Lord Jesus Christ will have come the second time and separated the wheat from the chaff for ever.' With many of his fellow evangelicals he believed that 'the second coming of our Lord Jesus Christ will be a real, literal, personal, bodily coming' and that the Jews would be restored to their own land and converted to faith in Christ. Though Ryle was convinced that Jesus' return would be sudden, he was against predicting precisely when it would take place, and challenged Christians to 'live as if you thought Christ might come at any time.'

One day in seven

The fourth of the Ten Commandments is 'remember the Sabbath day, to keep it holy' (Exodus 20:8) and Ryle wrote nearly twenty tracts on the subject. Sunday was a holy day, a day of rest, and intended for the benefit of all mankind. He believed that Sunday observance

Above: The new pulpit in All Saints, Stradbroke was put in place during the restoration of 1872

was fundamental to biblical Christianity and that Sabbath-breaking was sure proof of 'the low state of vital religion' and disunity among Christians; it was like a cancer 'eating into the heart of the Protestant churches.'

The day of rest was desecrated and steadily eroded away by running railway trains and steamboats, and employing 'clerks, porters, ticket-takers, policemen, guards, engine-drivers, stokers [and] omnibus drivers.' For Ryle it was wrong to adopt a Continental Sabbath characterized by 'pleasure-seeking [and] exhibition visiting' and so he challenged all Sabbath-breakers to read the Bible, to attend a place of worship, and to take time out during the week. He did not admire 'a gloomy religion … a day of sadness and unhappiness … I want everyone to regard Sunday as the brightest, cheerfullest day of all the seven.' Sunday was nothing less than 'a foretaste and fragment of heaven.'

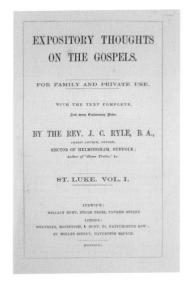

EXPOSITORY THOUGHTS
ON THE GOSPELS.

FOR FAMILY AND PRIVATE USE.

WITH THE TEXT COMPLETE.

And many Explanatory Notes.

BY THE REV. J. C. RYLE, B. A.,
CHRIST CHURCH, OXFORD.
RECTOR OF HELMINGHAM, SUFFOLK;
Author of "Home Truths," &c.

ST. LUKE. VOL. I.

IPSWICH:
WILLIAM HUNT, STEAM PRESS, TAVERN STREET.
LONDON:
WERTHEIM, MACINTOSH, & HUNT, 24, PATERNOSTER ROW;
22, HOLLES STREET, CAVENDISH SQUARE.

Above: Ryle's seven volumes of Expository Thoughts on the Gospels *were published between 1856 and 1873. For him 'the gospels were written to make us acquainted with Christ'*

Commentaries and hymns

In 1856, while at Helmingham, Ryle published the first of his *Expository Thoughts* on the four gospels and he completed them at Stradbroke in 1873. They first appeared as a series of monthly *Expository Tracts,* and in preparing them Ryle had three groups of readers in mind: First, for reading at family prayers; second, for those who visited the

Above: *The Baptist leader Charles Spurgeon (1845–1892) commended Ryle's* Expository Thoughts. *'We prize these volumes … Mr Ryle has evidently studied all previous writers upon the gospels and has given forth an individual utterance of considerable value'*

sick and the poor; and third, for private reading. His aim was clear. He wanted to lead his readers 'to Christ and faith in him, to repentance and holiness, to the Bible and to prayer.' His writing was the fruit 'of much work, much reading, much reflection and not a little prayer.' He consulted

over seventy commentators, yet he made it clear that 'I have set down nothing but what I conscientiously believe to be the real meaning of the inspired writer, and the mind of the Spirit.'

Ryle's doctrinal position was clear: 'my conviction is firm and decided, that the theology of that religious school in the Church of England, which, rightly or wrongly, is called evangelical, is thoroughly scriptural, and a theology of which no Christian man need be ashamed.' He believed in 'the plenary verbal inspiration of the Bible' and held to the view 'not only that the Bible *contains* the Word of God, but that every jot of it was written, or brought together, by divine inspiration, and *is* the Word of God'—a healthy and necessary distinction.

In the 19th century many clergy published their own collections of hymns and in this Ryle was no exception. At Helmingham he published one hundred *Spiritual Songs,* and later expanded the collection as *Hymns for the Church on Earth.* Unusually his hymn-books were not primarily intended for congregational use, but for 'the comfort of invalids and the edification of Christians in private', and to this end he quoted hymns in his tracts. Ryle believed that there were very few good hymn-writers. Many hymns may be sound and scriptural but they are at best 'tame, pointless, weak and milk and watery.' In his opinion there were 'not more than 200 first-rate hymns in the English language' and those composed by Augustus Toplady were some of

the best. The two of his hymns that Ryle most admired were 'A debtor to mercy alone' and (later sung at his funeral) 'Rock of ages, cleft for me'.

'Do not forsake the old paths'

Over and against the novelties of the Oxford Movement (and its successor, Anglo-Catholicism) and the impact of liberal theology, Ryle constantly urged evangelicals to 'stand fast on old principles. Do not forsake the old paths' never 'be ashamed of the old paths.' For Ryle, the 'old paths' represented the biblical, reformed, protestant faith and though despised and criticized it was the 'more excellent way' from which he had 'no reason to depart.' 'The longer I live', he wrote, 'the more I am convinced that the world needs no new gospel … but a bold, full, unflinching teaching of the "old paths".'

There was no new doctrine in his book *Old Paths*. The teaching was that of the 'simple, unadulterated, old-fashioned evangelical theology … in which the apostolic Christians, the Reformers, the best English churchmen for the last three hundred years, and the best evangelical Christians of the present day, have persistently walked.' He urged his fellow clergy to keep to 'the old paths. Walk

Left: The present Orange Street Chapel (very near the National Portrait Gallery) is on the site of the chapel where Toplady had been the minister and where it is believed 'Rock of Ages' was first sung

in them steadily. Make much of Christ. Pray continually for the quickening influences of the Holy Spirit ... work on steadily on these lines, and you will live to see miraculous changes.'

The Church of England

Ryle was wholly committed to the doctrinal principles of the Church of England and in his works often made reference to the *Book of Common Prayer*, the *Thirty-Nine Articles of Religion* and the *Homilies* (or sermons). Without these 'limits to comprehensiveness' the church would 'become a kind of Noah's ark' in which people could believe anything they wished. It was never intended that the Church of England would embrace 'men who preached downright popery on one side and on the other those who denied portions of scripture and spoke lightly of the atonement and the eternity of punishment.' Rather, 'let us be as broad as the Creeds and Articles, but not one inch broader.' Ryle made it clear that: 'we are convinced that the reformed Church of England, whatever people may say to the contrary, was intended to be a Protestant and an Evangelical church.' But unless it was further reformed it would be like 'some fossilized country squire who lives twenty miles from a railway and never visits London ... [and] must still travel in the old family coach, shoot with the old flint-locked single-barrel gun, and wear the old jack-boots and long pigtail.' It was the 'want of elasticity' the 'morbid dread of change, cast-iron stiffness, frozen inability to adapt' that had been the plague of the Church of England.

Though Ryle strongly supported the principle of the established church he was prepared to make some radical proposals for church reform. These included reducing the size of the dioceses; each bishop to receive an annual stipend of £2,000; only four or five bishops in the House of Lords; the bishops to be responsible for cathedrals (instead of deans) and to be assisted by four clergy. To assist parochial clergy he wanted to revive the ancient office of sub-deacon and to appoint evangelists; he also wanted to reduce the length of Sunday services, to hold non-liturgical services in unconsecrated buildings; and to make greater use of lay members of the church, sitting on a Bishops' Council, as members of local church councils, and local and national synods, and representing all shades of opinion within the church. Ryle maintained that 'church reform is one of the best bulwarks against church disestablishment.'

For Ryle, the true church consisted of God's elect, converted men and women, who were born again by the Holy Spirit. Such a church was not dependent upon forms, ceremonies, ordinances and buildings, but was united, holy, catholic and apostolic, and no one denomination could claim to be the true church. While he valued having bishops, he accepted that nonconformist ministers were real ministers of Jesus Christ.

Right: Lambeth Palace, on the south bank of the River Thames opposite the Houses of Parliament, is the official London residence of the Archbishop of Canterbury

Ryle concluded: 'True religion does not turn on Episcopacy or Presbyterianism, on churches or chapels, on liturgies or extempore prayer; but on justification, and sanctification, on saving faith and new hearts!' Disunity between Christians was a disgrace and Ryle wanted to see more unity between denominations. Apart from matters of 'sound doctrine', he urged the Church of England to make concessions towards nonconformists: 'If we cannot remove the hedges which separate us, let us keep them as low as we can, and shake hands over them.' However at the same time he was far less charitable towards Roman Catholicism which he believed to be in serious error and was nothing less than the anti-Christ.

English Reformers and Puritans

Ryle believed that over and against the Roman Catholic Church there were three great principles of the Protestant Reformation: the sufficiency of Holy Scripture, the right of private judgement, and justification by faith alone. He supported the theological principles of the Reformation, and admired the zeal of the Protestant Reformers. The Reformation brought about 'the regeneration of the Church of England' and, he believed that 'we are thoroughly in accord and harmony with Cranmer, Ridley, Hooper, Latimer and Jewel, as Protestant Evangelical members of the Church of England.' In *Facts and Men* Ryle wrote a series of biographies of the 16th century English Reformers as well as figures from the 17th century, and while the biographies may not be particularly academic they are good introductions to some of the leaders of the English church.

Left: Thomas Cranmer (1489–1556) the Archbishop of Canterbury from 1532 to 1556 took a leading role in the composition of The Book of Common Prayer *published in 1549 and 1552 (the basis of the later Prayer Book published in 1662)*

Three of Ryle's biographies were connected with East Anglia. In *Facts and Men* he wrote 'From the day that I was transplanted into the eastern counties, and became a Suffolk incumbent, I have made it my business to study the lives of eminent Suffolk divines.' The three Suffolk saints were the Reformer, Rowland Taylor, burned at the stake at Hadleigh in February 1555 (see in this series *The Martyrs of Mary Tudor* by Andrew Atherstone), and the Puritans Samuel Ward (1577–1639) of Ipswich, and William Gurnall (1616–1679) of Lavenham. Ryle loved and honoured the Puritans for 'their bold and outspoken Protestantism' and 'their clear, sharply-cut, distinct evangelicalism.' He was very familiar with their writings and frequently quoted from the words of Samuel Rutherford and John Bunyan. Ryle was a Puritan through and through, and in matters of practical theology and personal devotion, he had a simple maxim: 'the old is better'.

Revival and holiness

Ryle wrote a series of biographies on some of the leaders of the 18th century evangelical revival: well known figures like George Whitefield and John Wesley, and others less well known like John Berridge and James Hervey. Ryle made it clear that he was 'an enthusiastic admirer of the men whose pictures I have sketched' and it was his earnest prayer that God would 'raise up in his church men like those who are here described ... O Lord, revive thy work!' He was convinced 'that we want nothing new, no new systems, no new school of teaching, no new theology, no new ceremonial, no new gospel. We want nothing but the old truths rightly preached and rightly brought home to consciences, minds and wills. The evangelical system of theology revived England in the 18th century, and I have faith to believe that it could revive it again.'

During the 19th century a highly contentious issue was Christian holiness. This international and interdenominational movement emerged from the teaching of the American revivalist Charles Finney and it received added impetus by the teaching on the 'higher life' and in the perfectionist emphasis at Christian gatherings such as the Mildmay Conferences and the Keswick Convention. While Ryle supported the American evangelist Dwight L Moody and singer Ira D Sankey, he severely criticised the teaching of the revivalist Pearsall Smith—since, Ryle believed, they were as different as sunshine and fog!

Ryle was anxious to promote a form of biblical holiness that was progressive but not instantaneous. He did not think that 'sensational and exciting addresses by strange preachers or by women, loud singing, hot rooms, crowded

William Gurnall (1616–1679)

William Gurnall, who 'lived religion in every capacity', had been greatly influenced by the Puritans in his home town of King's Lynn and later when he was a student at Emmanuel College, Cambridge, where a number of like-minded Puritans were educated. After graduation Gurnall was ordained (probably as a Presbyterian minister) and possibly served as the minister at Sudbury, Suffolk before becoming the rector of Lavenham in 1644. At the time it was not uncommon for incumbents to be men who had not been ordained by a bishop. Gurnall was in post during the turbulent years of the Commonwealth, and after the restoration of the monarchy in 1660 he was one of the minority of 171 ministers in post who submitted to episcopal ordination, and thereby retained their incumbencies.

The Act of Uniformity of 1662 was, in Ryle's view, 'the crowning piece of folly' enacted by Charles II, and while Gurnall remained as a Church of England incumbent, about 1,800 of his fellow ministers who refused to conform had to leave their churches, colleges and schools. Just over half of the men who had been deprived of their freedom to preach the gospel were forced out of their homes, were subject to a vicious persecution by the authorities and became nonconformist ministers. Gurnall, who suffered from poor health, was a quiet retiring pastor known for his piety, humility, love and charity, and mainly for his book *The Christian in Complete Armour*. It was first published between 1655 and 1662, and is still in print today.

Below: When Moody and Sankey visited Eton College the young Herbert Ryle was not impressed.'"Soddy" preached not much different from what father would have done, except with slightly more coarseness, without heads and with rather longer stories and illustrations. "Mankey's" singing would sound better in a building than a garden, and otherwise I did not think much of it'

Dwight L Moody

Ira D Sankey

tents, the constant sight of strong semi-religious feeling in the faces of all around you for several days, late hours, long protracted meetings, public profession of experience' were conducive to scriptural holiness. Ryle was suspicious of mass meetings that appeared to be attractive and enthusiastic but did not produce a lasting change, and where 'mere animal excitement has been mistaken for the work of the Holy Spirit.' Not one to mince his words, Ryle described such hysterical Christianity as being 'little better than spiritual dram-drinking'.

For Ryle, there was too much talk about 'consecration' but not enough about 'conversion'. He believed that 'faith in Christ is the root of all holiness.' Belief is *followed* by holiness, and 'until we believe we will not have a jot of holiness.' While it is scriptural to affirm that 'faith alone justifies' it is unscriptural to say that 'faith alone sanctifies', and scripture did not teach 'a literal perfection, a complete and entire freedom from sin, in thought, or word, or deed.' Perfectionism was 'a dangerous delusion' and 'entire consecration … a man-made invention.' For Ryle the teaching at the end of Romans 7 'is a literal, perfect, accurate, correct photograph of the experience of every true servant of God.' The Bible only speaks about believers and unbelievers, the living and the dead and not the unconverted, the converted and those enjoying the 'higher life'. The Christian life is 'a holy violence, a conflict, a warfare, a fight' and any teaching about sanctification that denies personal exertion is false. It was to counter falsehood that Ryle published *Holiness. Its nature, hindrances, difficulties and roots.*

KEY
1 Norwich
2 Great Yarmouth
3 Lowestoft
4 Stradbroke
5 Framlingham
6 Stonham Aspal
7 Helmingham
8 Lavenham
9 Hadleigh
10 Ipswich

A MAP OF PART OF SUFFOLK

Ryle preached in many of the churches in Suffolk and also spoke at numerous public meetings. On the A1120 and to the east of Helmingham is the hamlet of Stonham Aspal. There the evangelical rector Charles Shorting was one of Ryle's closest friends, and each year he convened a large gathering of the supporters of the Church Missionary Society. About 800 people came from the area and met in a large tent erected in the rectory grounds. To the north-west of Stonham Aspal (off the B1113) is Old Newton where another of Ryle's fellow evangelicals Charles Bridges was the vicar. He was a distinguished commentator and author of *The Christian Ministry*.

Often Ryle was in Ipswich and spoke at missionary and philanthropic meetings in the Town Hall and Corn Hall, and over the years he preached in most of the town's churches. There were also large attendances when Ryle preached to the working classes at St Clement's. Three of Ryle's Suffolk biographies are associated with the area. In Ipswich the vicar of St Mary-le-Tower was the Puritan Samuel Ward; and to the west on the A1071 is Hadleigh where the reformer Rowland Taylor was burned at the stake 1555. Next to the parish church is Hadleigh Tower where, in July 1833, some of the early promoters of the Oxford Movement held a conference. On the A1141 to the north-west of Hadleigh is Lavenham where William Gurnall was the vicar of the parish church. The small towns of Lavenham and Hadleigh are well worth visiting.

❼ Popular preacher

Outside his country parishes J C Ryle was a much sought after preacher and popular speaker. This brought him into public prominence which was to his advantage when the Prime Minister appointed the first Bishop of Liverpool

How was it that after ten years in an obscure Suffolk parish Ryle was being invited to address numerous regional, national and evangelical meetings? There were a number of reasons for his rise to prominence. First, in the publication of his many popular tracts, second, in meeting the many well-connected visitors to Helmingham Hall, and third, when his second wife needed specialist medical treatment in the capital, Ryle was invited to preach in some sixty London churches. Yet at the same time he shunned popularity and believed that it was bad for the soul: 'Why I was popular I really do not know, for I am certain that my preaching was very inferior to what it was after I was turned fifty. But it was always bold and aggressive and downright, and I suppose was very unlike what London congregations generally heard, and therefore was popular.'

Addressing non-evangelicals and evangelicals

Ryle believed that evangelicals ought to contend for the faith and to be active outside their parishes. In 1865 he attended his first Church Congress in Norwich and spoke in the discussion on preaching. The Congress was an annual gathering of upwards of 2,500 clergy and laity representing all shades of opinion within the Church of England, and this prompted him to ask, 'Am I right or am I wrong in being here?' Initially he attended out of a sense of duty but it gave him the opportunity to engage face to face with those who held different opinions. While many evangelical clergy deliberately refused to meet

Above: *Onslow Square, London was the home of John Johnston the uncle of Jessie Ryle, where her unnamed premature daughter was born and soon died in January 1853*

Facing page: *Exeter Hall, 372 The Strand, London, had an inscription in Greek above the door —'Loving brothers'*

Above: Borrowdale Hotel, three miles south of Keswick, where Ryle suggested that the clergy of the Church of England should meet together to discuss their differences. The hotel, which was built in 1866, was probably already known to Ryle since he was a frequent visitor to the Lake District

with their opponents, Ryle had no such hesitation, and from 1868 he spoke at thirteen Congresses held throughout England, Wales and Ireland. He spoke on a variety of topics: church and state, Christian unity, the reform of Convocation, church and dissent, and the spiritual life. Through his presence and contribution he gained the reputation of being one of the leading evangelical spokesmen. In 1870 it was said that Ryle 'laid the foundation at Southampton of the remarkable popularity he enjoyed for many years as a Congress speaker, his *bonhomie* making his hard-hitting agreeable even to those whom he vigorously but good-humouredly (may I say) pummelled.' He was a powerful speaker—'fluent, forcible and effective' to a remarkable degree.

However, not everyone approved of his involvement in the Congresses, and he was criticised by some evangelicals who daubed John Ryle, Edward Garbett and Edward Hoare as 'neo-evangelicals' for mixing with non-evangelicals. Ryle responded to his critics in a tract called 'Shall we go?' and blamed his fellow evangelicals for misjudging High Churchmen. He positively urged unity in the church and joked that he had not caught any theological disease from associating with those with whom he disagreed! Rather than criticising each other from afar he suggested bringing together the different factions. Take them away to the Borrowdale Hotel, south of Derwentwater in the Lake District, and isolate them from letters and newspapers, and 'give them nothing but their Bibles, their Prayer Books, pens, ink and paper, and ask them to talk matters over quietly among themselves, to find out wherein they differed and wherein they agreed, and to put it down in black and white.' The outcome, he believed, 'would bring to light clear evidence of a vast amount of unity.' But while such a meeting may have been highly profitable to all concerned there is no evidence to suggest that it ever took place.

Eugene Stock, the evangelical historian, supported Ryle's involvement: 'Canon Ryle was throughout [the 1870s] perhaps the most prominent and honoured of the evangelical leaders … Mr Ryle was admired, not only for his staunchness to evangelical truth, but for his independence of mind; and at the Church Congresses his popularity was great with all parties. His letters to the *Record* [newspaper] on church reform were too bold to win assent from his brethren generally, who were more afraid than he was of changes and innovations; yet the fact of his having the courage to write them added to his significance.'

As an engaging and effective speaker Ryle was often invited to address meetings of the leading Anglican Evangelical societies. Some of his sermons and addresses to these bodies were published as tracts and later included in his books. He was also called upon to address interdenominational societies and spoke on numerous occasions to the British and Foreign Bible Society and to the London City Mission. Ryle saw the Church Pastoral Aid Society as providing 'light-houses to guide souls to the haven of everlasting peace', and the 'glorious institution, the London City Mission' to be like a life-boat rescuing ship-wrecked souls.'

Above: The 19th century headquarters of the Church Missionary Society

Mission overseas and mission at home

The Church Missionary Society (CMS) was founded by Anglican Evangelicals in 1799. Each year an annual sermon was preached to its supporters and in 1862 it was delivered by Ryle. Of this address it was said that 'his sermon is one of those perfectly plain, terse, incisive addresses with which the whole Church of England has since become so familiar.' Following the publication of the controversial book *Essays and Reviews,* Ryle contrasted the fruit of the CMS missionaries with the barrenness of the Broad Church party. The former rejoiced 'bringing their sheaves with them' (Psalm 126:6)—like the first Nigerian bishop, Samuel Crowther—but where were the equivalent sheaves from the liberal churchmen?

Throughout his ministry Ryle actively supported the CMS and frequently spoke at the annual meetings in Exeter Hall. To mark the centenary of CMS in 1899, fourteen meetings were held throughout London. At a meeting chaired by Ryle in the Queen's Hall, he emphasised 'the Society's faithfulness to its evangelical and spiritual principles.' After his death, Eugene Stock referred to Ryle as being 'a very staunch friend and supporter of the Society, though his residence far from London, both as rector and as bishop, prevented his ever taking an active part in its councils. His influence as a leading representative of the evangelical section of the church is frequently referred to in the [History of the] CMS.'

The interdenominational London Society for Promoting Christianity amongst the Jews founded in 1809 became wholly Anglican in 1815. Ryle was very supportive of the conversion of the Jews and became an active

Above: Samuel Adjai Crowther (c.1806–1891) who was kidnapped as a boy and later, following his conversion to Christianity, became a teacher and missionary. He was ordained in 1843, and in 1864 became the Bishop of Niger in West Africa

Right: St Bride's church, Fleet Street, London where the annual sermons of the Church Missionary Society were preached. It was an important occasion and a great compliment to be invited to preach at what was considered to be 'the blue riband (ribbon) of the Evangelical pulpit'

Above: St Mary and St Lambert, Stonham Aspal, Suffolk where J C Ryle's close friend, Charles Shorting, was the evangelical rector

member of the Society. He preached two annual sermons, spoke at five annual meetings, and to numerous meetings outside London, and in 1875 became an honorary life governor. His sermon 'Scattered and gathered' preached in 1858 was published as a tract, and translated into German.

The Church Pastoral Aid Society (CPAS) was founded by Anglican Evangelicals in 1836 to provide support for clergy and lay workers, many of whom were intending to be ordained, to work in evangelical parishes. Ryle was a dedicated supporter of CPAS and addressed the annual meeting on numerous occasions and preached two of the annual sermons to the supporters.

Though he served in the country, Ryle was all too aware of the great needs in the cities. In an alley in a London parish he found 'as many people residing there as are inhabitants in the whole of my parish in Suffolk' and where the minister was expected to be responsible for 25,000 to 30,000 people. Ryle questioned those he met: 'when did a minister or clergyman come to visit you?' One woman replied that in the past twelve years she had been visited by lay visitors or London City missioners, but never by a clergyman. But Ryle did not condemn the urban clergy since they were overburdened with baptisms, marriages and funerals, sermon preparation and visiting the sick, and had no time left to visit the healthy and to spread the gospel.

In May 1850 Ryle addressed the annual meeting of the CPAS. Fifteen years before this, men had questioned whether the Church of England had any future, but now the situation had changed. There

Above: The annual meeting of the local CMS took place in a large tent in the grounds of Stoneham Aspal rectory

was much activity, and more churches and chapels had been built. But 'if new churches are not built for the accommodation of the increasing population; if clergymen are not sent among the people to preach the gospel; if schools are not provided for the young, and lay-agents sent amongst the people in the large towns, to bring them into Christ's fold, we have no right to expect anything but infidelity, ignorance, superstition and sin.' If ignored, then socialism, Mormonism and infidelity would spread and many people would seek salvation outside the Church of England. Though, he had to admit, it was far better 'for men to be uncanonically saved than canonically lost' and that 'the ministers of the Church of England should never speak unkindly of dissenters.'

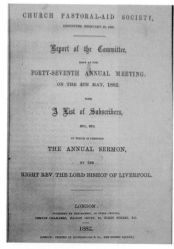

Above: In 1868 and 1882 Ryle preached the annual sermon to the supporters of the Church Pastoral Aid Society

Ryle believed that the CPAS had the responsibility to maintain and promote 'the pure old principles of the Reformation' and that its supporters were 'true churchmen'. It was his

Above: *The centre of the London Society for Promoting Christianity amongst the Jews was Palestine Place, Cambridge Heath Road, Bethnal Green, London. On the five acre site was a missionary college, a chapel, schools for boys and girls, workshops for converted Jews and private houses. In 1895 the site was sold and the large Bethnal Green Infirmary was opened in 1900. After the hospital was closed in 1990 the site was redeveloped for housing*

conviction that 'what we want is the simple announcement of the gospel of Jesus Christ' with 'Christ crucified, the only hope of salvation' at the centre, and all else subordinate to it. The teaching of the Church of England was challenged *externally* by infidelity, Roman Catholicism and Mormonism, and *internally* by Tractarianism—'that bye-path to Rome'—and by a liberal version of Christianity that denied the inspiration of scripture and the substitutionary atonement. Both false teaching and Sabbath

Right: *St Dunstan-in-the-West, Fleet Street, London where the annual sermons of the Church Pastoral Aid Society were preached. From 1842 to 1880 the highly respected rector was the evangelical leader Edward Auriol (1805–1880)*

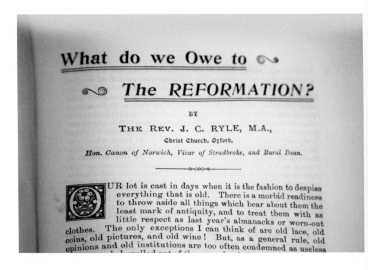

Above: The tract What do we owe to the Reformation? *was first published in 1877*

breaking needed to be challenged and more clergy were required particularly in the large, urban parishes. The solution was to reduce the size of large parishes, to increase the number of clergy and to provide lay-workers. They 'must go about with clear, positive and distinctive doctrines' and be prepared to answer questions like: 'How can I be just with God? How can I have peace with God? How can I have my sins taken away? How can I face death, and have its sting removed? Where shall I stand in the judgement day?' Their response must be 'distinctive and positive … Protestant and Evangelical.'

Challenging the ritualists

In 1865 the Church Association (CA) was founded to confront the growing excesses of ritualism in the Church of England. The Anglo-Catholic clergy were a law unto themselves and members of the CA confronted what they considered to be an attempt to undermine the Protestant and Reformed principles of the Church of England. The practices of the ritualistic clergy were challenged in the courts of law to establish the illegality of their teaching and practices. From the outset Ryle was thoroughly involved with the CA and became a vice-president in 1870. He spoke at national and regional gatherings and for over ten years was a leading speaker and several of his addresses were published as CA tracts. But on becoming a bishop he distanced himself from the Society by resigning his membership.

Throughout the country the CA had a significant body of lay and clerical supporters, and Ryle believed that it was 'a fulcrum for

Left: Under successive incumbents St Mary's parish church, Islington became the centre of London evangelicalism. In time it seeded a number of evangelical parishes, and nearby were colleges to train evangelical missionaries, teachers and clergy. By the 1880s the annual Islington Clerical Meeting attracted 300 and 400 evangelical clergy

shaking the country, and uniting all Evangelical churchmen' and, 'I know of no better organization than that of the Church Association.'

It was important to inform the public that the CA was not involved with wrangles 'about unimportant ceremonial trifles, but to resist things which are the stepping-stones to popery.'

The Church Association

When it was formed in 1865 the CA had two clear aims, to uphold the Protestant principles of the Church of England and to counteract the teaching and ritualistic practices of Anglo-Catholic clergy. Those who opposed the Association referred to it as the 'Persecution Society Ltd' but its supporters believed it was primarily for defence but not defiance. Ryle urged his fellow evangelicals to unite behind the CA, but as the years passed its aggressive stance made this impossible, and other less militant bodies like CPAS were better placed to draw evangelicals together.

Throughout the country there were about 100 local branches of the CA and with a membership of over 9,500. The wider public were informed about its activities through meetings and the publication of more than 400 tracts, ten of which were by Ryle. In the first eighteen years of the Association, 1,450,000 tracts were published, and in one year 88,000 copies of Ryle's tract 'What do we owe to the Reformation?' were sold. The CA *Monthly Intelligencer* had a circulation of 12,000 copies.

Through the courts of law the Association sought to determine what practices in Church of England services were legal or illegal. By 1877 it was established that fifty-nine matters were illegal, and over £52,000 was raised as a Guarantee Fund to meet legal fees. But ritualistic court cases were expensive, counter-productive and divisive and were not the best way of winning friends or promoting the gospel, and by the early 1890s they were dropped.

Left: St Martin's church, Birmingham where the evangelical John Miller (1814–1880) was the rector from 1846 to 1866

Preaching to clergy and the working classes

On a number of occasions Ryle addressed gatherings of evangelical clergy in Islington, London and in Weston-super-Mare, Somerset. From 1849 Archdeacon Henry Law convened an annual meeting of three hundred or so clergy at Weston-super-Mare. Ryle attended at least four of these gatherings and delivered eight addresses. In 1858 one of the clergy present noted that 'Ryle preached a noble sermon last night on the text

Below: Ryle had exceptionally poor hand-writing

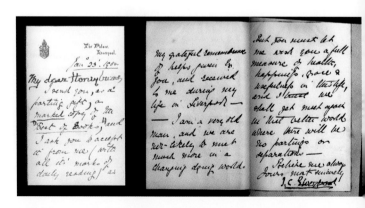

Above: Ryle's preaching Bible was in use from 1878 to 1881

"Upon this rock I will build my church; and the gates of hell shall not prevail against it" [Matthew 16:18] which was listened to with deep attention for an hour and a half.'

In November 1856 three evangelical clergy, Hugh McNeile, John Miller and John Ryle preached a series of week-night sermons to 2,000 of the working classes in St Martin's church, Birmingham, and the local paper reported that the services were simple and solemn.' This prompted similar services to be held throughout the country (including Ipswich and Lowestoft in Suffolk) and in Exeter Hall, London, where Ryle preached in June 1857 and August 1858. However, after objections from the incumbent of the parish in which the Hall was situated, the services were held elsewhere until a change in the law permitted them to take place in unconsecrated buildings. But no such legalities prevented preaching services for

Right: The site of Exeter Hall is now occupied by the Strand Palace Hotel

Exeter Hall, London

Known as 'The great evangelical temple', Exeter Hall, situated in The Strand, was opened in 1831 at a cost of £30,000. Though the main entrance was modest, the inside of the building was extensive and included a number of committee rooms, offices and three large halls, one of which could seat over 3,000 people. To address such large numbers without any amplification must have been very demanding for the platform speakers and difficult for the hearers.

Every year, from April to June, Exeter Hall was the venue for the famous 'May meetings' of evangelical missionary and philanthropic societies. At first about thirty annual meetings were held but in time there were over four hundred, and sometimes as many as twenty-two different meetings were held on the same day. As well as a venue for evangelical gatherings, Exeter Hall was used for temperance meetings, concerts, sacred oratorios and as a centre for teaching day and Sunday school teachers how to sing. Until the Royal Albert Hall was built, Exeter Hall was the musical centre of the capital. Ryle echoed the view that Exeter Hall was the 'fifth estate' alongside the monarch, the House of Lords, the House of Commons and the *Times* newspaper.

From 1845 the YMCA promoted the Exeter Hall Lectures, and in 1855 the Baptist leader, Charles Spurgeon held services there while his chapel was being enlarged. Exeter Hall was acquired by the YMCA for £25,000 and reopened by them in 1881. The building was demolished in 1907 and became the site of The Strand Palace Hotel.

Above: The rooms in Exeter Hall could accommodate large numbers of people

the working classes being held in Westminster Abbey and St Paul's Cathedral.

On three occasions Ryle addressed congregations of 'working men' (and once to women) at fringe meetings of the Church Congresses, and on other occasions he and other evangelicals were invited to address George Moore's employees in London. It was Ryle's conviction 'that our working classes want nothing more nor less than the old gospel of our Lord and Saviour.'

TRAVEL INFORMATION

After graduating from Oxford, Ryle spent a year and a half in London. There he tried his hand at the law in chambers in Lincoln's Inn and lodged in Pall Mall and worshipped at St John's, Bedford Row (later demolished). When he was a Suffolk incumbent he preached in some sixty London churches, including two in Fleet Street—St Bride's and St Dunstan-in-the-West. He was a frequent speaker at meetings at Exeter Hall, The Strand where he addressed the working classes and also at Westminster Abbey.

On the south bank of the nearby River Thames is Lambeth Palace, the official London residence of the Archbishop of Canterbury. Within the grounds is the Lambeth Palace Library which has a collection of almost 200,000 printed books and nearly 5,000 manuscripts. The library is open to the public and no appointment is needed but for a reader's ticket identification is required. Open Monday to Friday 10.00am to 5.00pm.

Lambeth Palace Library
London SE1 7JU
www.Lambethpalacelibrary.org

Below: *Dean Ryle Street, Westminster was named after J C Ryle's second son, Bishop Herbert Ryle*

Right: *Westminster Abbey where Bishop Herbert Ryle was the dean from 1911 until his death in 1925. There are two memorials to him—one on the floor near the tomb of the Unknown Warrior and the other on a nearby wall*

8 The first Bishop of Liverpool

Moving from rural Suffolk to an industrial city of more than half a million people must have been a considerable culture shock to J C Ryle and his family. However as the first Bishop of Liverpool he faced new responsibilities and had the opportunity to promote the gospel in an urban situation

In March 1880 Ryle was unexpectedly nominated to become the Dean of Salisbury, and in spite of his reservations he believed that it was his duty to go. However, events soon took an unexpected turn. The following month Ryle received a telegram inviting him to meet the Conservative Prime Minister, Benjamin Disraeli. Ryle was met at the station by Lord Sandon, one of the Liverpool MPs, who asked him whether or not he would accept the bishopric of Liverpool. An immediate response was necessary for in the following week the government would be out of office, and with the prospect of William Gladstone as Prime Minister, an Anglo-Catholic would certainly be appointed to the new diocese.

Though Ryle protested that he was neither young nor wealthy, without any hesitation he replied, 'my Lord, I will go', and believed that he 'would much rather wear out as Bishop of Liverpool, than rust out as Dean of Salisbury.' On being introduced to Disraeli, Ryle repeated that he was not a young man, but Disraeli looked him up and down and said, 'I think, sir, you have a good constitution.'

On returning home Ryle broke the news to his wife. Henrietta told their housekeeper, who told the village gossip, and soon everyone knew. The next day the church bells of Stradbroke rang out in celebration.

'A Protestant bishop'
Shortly before his consecration Ryle had made it clear that he would not be 'a milk and water bishop, a colourless bishop, without any opinion at all.' He later commented that 'the flag which I have raised for these thirty years past I do not mean to haul down or to lower for one moment.' At the same time he did not see himself as the bishop of a particular party, but would 'hold out the right hand to all loyal churchmen, by whatever name they like to call themselves.'

Facing page: The first Bishop of Liverpool from 1880 to 1900. Ryle believed that 'the bishop of a new diocese has the greatest need of patience. He cannot command success all at once, and must be content to do the work of a sower, and wait'

Above: 19 Abercromby Square was the Bishops' Palace until it was bought by the University of Liverpool in the 1920s

In May 1880 he became 'Dr Ryle' when he was awarded an honorary DD from the University of Oxford, and the following month he was consecrated as a bishop in York Minster. The sermon, preached by his old friend Edward Garbett, was on the text, 'He was a good man, and full of the Holy Spirit and of faith' (Acts 11:24). Bishop Ryle refused the customary pastoral staff, cope and mitre, saying that he did not want to make a guy of himself.

The new diocese of Liverpool, carved out of the diocese of Chester, was geographically compact, and with a population of 1,085,634—about a half of whom lived within the parliamentary boundary of Liverpool. Publications of the day referred to 'squalid Liverpool' where the very wealthy lived in close proximity to the poorest of the poor in overcrowded slums. Outside the city there were urban centres like Bootle, Garston, Ormskirk, Prescot, St Helens, Southport, Warrington, Widnes and Wigan.

An endowment of £100,000 was created to establish the new diocese and 19 Abercromby Square was purchased as the bishops' residence. The diocese was divided into the two archdeaconries of Liverpool and Warrington, and sub-divided into nine (later eleven) deaneries. The clergy and laity from each deanery met twice a year, and the annual diocesan conference included every clergyman and two lay representatives from each parish.

Below: A caricature of Bishop J C Ryle (Vanity Fair, 26 March 1881)

Living agents

Long before he became a bishop, Ryle believed that the priority for urban areas was to appoint 'the living agents first; [then] bricks and mortar afterwards.' By living agents he meant 'missionary curates, Scripture Readers, lay-agents, Bible-women, and voluntary lay-helpers.' In Liverpool, the priority was to increase the

Right: On 11 June 1880, before a large congregation in York Minster, Ryle was consecrated as a bishop

number of clergy and to create manageable sized parishes. Since it was unreasonable to expect a clergyman to be responsible for upwards of 30,000 people, the bishop wanted each parish to have no more than 5,000 residents. Ryle was keen to encourage more 'right-minded living agents' to work in the parishes, and 'try to get ordained helpers if you can and lay-agents if you cannot.' During his episcopate the number of clergy increased from 275 in 1880 to 431 in 1900, and lay men and women were appointed as Scripture Readers, lay readers, Church Army officers and Bible women.

The bishop insisted that those men who were ordained in his diocese were selected after a rigorous examination, and candidates who were doctrinally unsound were rejected. Ryle led a three-day retreat for the candidates at Abercromby Square, and as soon as they arrived he made certain things clear: 'now remember, while you are in my house I expect you to behave like gentlemen. No smoking. Let us pray …'. He ordained 555 men as deacons and all but four were ordained as priests, and he invited those whom he had ordained to his annual 'presbyters' parties'.

Ryle recognised the value of 'the ordinance of confirmation' and while it was not essential to salvation, it followed closely behind preaching and the administration of the sacraments. It was his view that the preparation of the candidates provided an important point of contact between the clergy and those being confirmed. Each year, on average there were 6,000 to 7,000 candidates, and during his episcopate Ryle confirmed 133,947 individuals from the age of 15 and upwards. He discouraged holding confirmation services on a Sunday, because a long service would reduce the length of the sermon, for 'a bishop is not intended to confirm only, but to preach.'

While he welcomed the contribution of the nonconformist denominations, Ryle knew that the Church of England had failed to keep pace

Above: Bishop J C Ryle, 'a Christian champion of Protestant truth'

with the rising population, and he was anxious to provide more places of worship. The design of the new buildings would be plain and simple and the expenses would be raised locally. In poor areas it was cheaper to open halls or rooms in which clergy could 'give short, elementary, non-liturgical services, such as the Apostles used to hold' and where laymen could officiate. He considered the 200 mission rooms to be 'stepping stones to the parish church.' During his episcopate forty-four churches were consecrated (see page 123) and fifty-one halls and rooms were licensed for worship.

Liverpool Cathedral
Although a cathedral was needed for the diocese, Ryle did not regard it as a priority: 'My first and foremost business … is to provide for preaching the gospel to souls now entirely neglected,

whom no cathedral would touch.' Smaller parishes were required before 'splendid Gothic cathedrals [were] to be built.' Ryle was as good as his word, and throughout his episcopate Liverpool parish church (St Peter's) in Church Street served as the pro-cathedral.

A competition to design the cathedral was launched but the site adjacent to St George's Hall was unpopular and the fund-raising was dogged by economic recession. Over the course of the next three years it was concluded that 'the scheme is now at a complete standstill' and for the time being the project was abandoned. The failure to erect a cathedral was a personal disappointment to Ryle and it provided another excuse for his opponents to criticise him.

In 1901, with a new bishop (Francis Chavasse), a new site (St James' Mount) and a new

Above: 'Little Hell' a very poor part of Windsor, Liverpool

Right: In April 1898 Emmanuel church, Southport was the last church to be consecrated by Bishop Ryle

architect (Giles Gilbert Scott) the project to erect a new cathedral went ahead. On 19 July 1904 Edward VII laid the foundation stone and the Lady Chapel, the first part of the cathedral to be completed, was consecrated on St Peter's Day, 29 June 1910. Seventy-four years later on 25 October 1978 the completion of the building was marked by a service attended by Queen Elizabeth II.

Although building a cathedral was not a priority, Ryle was convinced that it was essential to have a Church House to accommodate the diocesan registry, offices for the bishop and his staff, committee and reading rooms and a diocesan library. However, fund-raising was again a problem, and as time passed Ryle doubted whether he would ever live to see it opened. He was unwell when the foundation stone was laid in August 1899, and had died before the building was opened by the Archbishop of York in May 1901.

On his death, Ryle left his 4,000 books to Church House, and the Bishop Ryle Library was opened by his son, Bishop Herbert Ryle. Unfortunately the building was hit during an air raid in May 1941 and the library and the diocesan records were destroyed.

St Nathaniel's, Windsor

On Sundays, the Ryle family and their servants attended St Nathaniel's church, Windsor (off Upper Parliament Street). The vicar, Richard Hobson, was a dedicated evangelical whom Ryle described as 'a quiet unpretending man ... a man who tries to preach Christ in the pulpit, and to visit his people in a Christ-like, sympathizing way as a pastor, at the rate of seventy-five families a week; and to these two things I attribute his success.'

Final publications and controversy

During his episcopate, Ryle composed fewer tracts, but a number of books, such as *Boys and Girls Playing* (addresses to children), *Facts and Men*, *Principles for Churchmen*, *Disestablishment Papers* and *The Upper Room* (which were mostly his episcopal sermons and addresses). Two posthumous publications were *The Christian*

Above and inset: St Peter's church was opened in June 1704, closed in 1919 and demolished in 1922, and the proceeds from the sale of the site was given to the endowment of the new cathedral. At the same time the church of Our Lady and St Nicholas became Liverpool parish church, within which St Peter's chapel contains the communion table from the former pro-cathedral

Race and other Sermons and his *Charges and Addresses.*

Ryle attended the Lambeth Conference of 1888 and served on a committee on Sunday observance. Part of the resolution concluded 'that the observance of the Lord's Day as a day of rest, of worship, and of religious teaching, has been a priceless blessing in all Christian lands in which it has been maintained; [and] that the growing laxity in its observance threatens a great change in its sacred and beneficent character.' At the same Conference Ryle was a member of the committee on the care of emigrants, particularly over their religious and moral welfare.

By the 1870s and 1880s ritualism had got out of hand and was, in Ryle's opinion, 'a dangerous system which ought to be exposed.' Many ritualistic priests were a law unto themselves and were not prepared to submit to the authority of their diocesan bishop, and the Public Worship Regulation Act of 1874 was an attempt to curb excessive ritualism. So called 'aggrieved parishioners' could object to ritualistic innovations in their parish church and charges could be brought against offending clergy. Those who refused to co-operate could be disciplined, and further down the line five clergy were actually imprisoned, one of whom was James Bell Cox, the vicar of St Margaret's, Toxteth.

While Cox's congregation was supportive of his practices Ryle made it perfectly clear that ritualism was not a matter to be decided by the congregation, but by law. It was Ryle's contention that while he upheld the law, it was Cox who broke it. Although Cox was prepared to give canonical obedience to his bishop, he was not prepared

Above: Church House, South John Street, Liverpool from 1901 to 1941

Richard Hobson (1831–1910)

Richard Hobson, an Irish evangelical and fervent Protestant, was the vicar of St Nathaniel, Windsor, Liverpool for thirty-three years. When he arrived it was a poor, working-class parish, a third of whom were Roman Catholics, and where only thirty families could afford to employ a domestic servant. There were sixteen public houses and two beer shops, and one street was known as 'Little Hell'. Initially Hobson began his ministry with five people in a cellar and then as numbers increased in a mission room. He worked tirelessly visiting six hours a day from Monday to Friday, and three hours on Saturday.

Throughout his ministry the teaching at St Nathaniel's was evangelical and Protestant and the services were 'plain, bright, hearty and congregational.' His goal was 'the spiritual

Inset: Richard Hobson was the vicar of St Nathaniel's church, Windsor from 1868 to 1901

regeneration of souls, and their sanctification, as seen in the life of faith, and of its outcome, good works.' In time, Hobson had the assistance of a curate, a Scripture Reader, a Bible-woman and an organist. There were 82 Sunday school teachers, 120 church workers, 600 adults in 17 Bible classes, and a Sunday school of 1,700 children. He built up the congregation so that by the early 1880s the church had the second highest attendance in Liverpool with 700 in the morning, 300 in the afternoon and 950 in the evening, and with 800 communicants. The impact upon his parish meant that there were 1,100 abstainers from alcohol and not a single brothel or known infidel.

to obey the dictates of a secular court. From July to October 1880 seventeen letters between Ryle and Cox were published, and brought matters to a head. Once Ryle had made it clear that he was not going to bring formal proceedings against Cox, members of the Liverpool branch of the Church Association took action to prosecute Cox for his numerous ritualistic

ST. NATHANIEL'S, WINDSOR.

Above: St Nathaniel's church, Windsor 'a plain brick church, holding 1,000' was opened in July 1869. It was rebuilt after a fire and after becoming redundant in June 1981 was demolished

irregularities. Throughout the case, Cox was supported by the English Church Union for the 'defence of the liberties and ritual of the Church of England.' Technically Ryle could have vetoed the prosecution, but in failing to do so was severely censured by his opponents. The eventual outcome was

that Cox refused to submit to the judgement of the secular authorities, and in May 1887 he was arrested and spent seventeen days in Walton Prison. He became something of a celebrity and each day of his imprisonment he received 500 to 600 letters of support. In 1892 a further attempt was made to curb his activities, but the proceedings were eventually dropped.

'That man of granite with the heart of a child'

Ryle's cousin recalled how Ryle took a daily walk along the dockside. He was always soberly dressed in black, wore boots, a hat and carried an umbrella in all weathers. A daughter of an archdeacon remembered seeing the bishop sitting in his carriage and on the opposite seat were his two dachshunds.

Henrietta Ryle, who was in poor health for the last three years of her life, died in April 1889 and her body was interred in the churchyard of All Saints, Childwall. Ten years later Ryle wrote, 'life has never been the same thing, or the world the same world, ever since my wife died' and for the rest of his life their unmarried daughter, Isabelle, acted as his personal assistant. Ryle, who suffered a minor stroke in 1891, was able to secure the assistance of Peter Royston the retired Bishop of Mauritius who, from 1891 to 1905, was the assistant bishop in the diocese and from 1896 the vicar of All Saints, Childwall.

When Herbert Ryle visited his father in September 1899

he found that he was unsteady on his feet, and suffering from deafness and loss of memory. When Herbert raised the matter of resigning his father was greatly relieved and pleased that someone had helped him to make up his mind, and within twenty-four hours he had sent his letter of resignation to the Archbishop of York. As a parting gift Ryle was presented with an illuminated address and a silver salver given by the clergy and laity of the diocese. He had planned to leave Liverpool early in March 1900 but was too frail to travel and remained in Abercromby Square until he and Isabelle moved to a large rented property in Kirkley Cliff Road, Lowestoft. The end came fairly soon and Isabelle was at her father's bedside when he died of a stroke on 10 June. The post mortem recorded that his death was caused by an 'atheroma of cerebral arteries serious effusion into the brain.'

His body was taken back to Liverpool where it was interred next to his wife at All Saints, Childwall. Herbert recorded that 'the church was filled with clergy and gentry. The graveyard was crowded with

James Bell Cox (1837–1923)

After serving two curacies James Bell Cox became the curate of St Margaret's, Toxteth, Liverpool. The first vicar, Charles Parnell, was a troublesome Anglo-Catholic ritualist and after a lengthy lawsuit he resigned in 1876 and was succeeded by his hard-working curate.

Soon after his appointment Ryle urged Cox to abandon the use of lighted candles on the communion table, the use of incense, and wearing a cope and biretta (all of which were illegal). The vicar was unrepentant and the bishop refused to license a second curate to St Margaret's. The differences between the bishop and the vicar continued and eventually resulted in Cox being imprisoned in Walton Prison. While publically they were poles apart, on a personal level Ryle and

Inset: *James Bell Cox*

Cox had a very amicable relationship and respected each other's deeply held convictions. An obituary notice said that Cox was 'a very loveable character, devout, sweet-natured, kindly-hearted, genial, most courteous and full of humour.'

In April 1904 a visitor to the church observed that there were lighted candles and a large stone crucifix; Cox wore a cream coloured chasuble, and two servers dressed in red cassocks, had lace trimmed albs with red girdles. Out of a congregation of 500, there were only three communicants, the others being observers rather than participants. Of the five clergy who were imprisoned for ritualism, Cox was the only one who remained in post after being released, and he defiantly continued to practice Anglo-Catholic ritual until he resigned in 1921.

Left:

Helmingham House, 58 Kirkley Cliff Road, Lowestoft where Ryle died in June 1900

poor people who had come in carts and vans and buses to pay the last honours to the old man—who certainly had won their love.' On his gravestone was his 'conversion' text—'By grace are ye saved through faith' (Ephesians 2:8)—and another that expressed something of his inner convictions: 'I have fought a good fight, I have finished my course, I have kept the faith' (2 Timothy 4:7).

Preaching after Ryle's funeral, Richard Hobson paid tribute to his friend, 'perhaps few men in the 19th century did so much for God, for truth, and for righteousness, among the English speaking race, and in the world, as our late bishop.' Bishop Francis Chavasse spoke warmly of his predecessor and referred to Ryle as 'that man of granite with the heart of a child, the man whose name is better known throughout that part of Christendom where the English language is spoken than that of any other except Charles Spurgeon.'

Postscript on Ryle's evangelicalism

Throughout his life, Ryle was not without his critics. The theology of his tracts was challenged by counter-tracts, his advocacy of

Right: The gravestones of John and Henrietta Ryle in the churchyard of All Saints' church, Childwall

Right: *Bishop Ryle's monument in the south choir aisle of Liverpool cathedral was unveiled in May 1933*

church reform was ignored, his commitment to the principles of the Church Association brought much criticism, his nomination to the deanery of Salisbury was not welcomed, and in becoming Bishop of Liverpool he received the approbation of the Anglo-Catholics. The *Church Times* predicted that he would 'be a very bad Bishop of Liverpool.' During his episcopate Ryle's Anglo-Catholic opponents were particularly critical of his handling of the events that led to the imprisonment of James Bell Cox, and those in Scotland were opposed to him confirming candidates from the 'English Chapels'. Herbert Ryle, observed that 'the high church writers deliberately sought to destroy his position by detraction.'

At the same time Ryle was criticised by the more hard-line Protestants who had denounced him for wearing a surplice in the pulpit instead of the traditional black preaching gown, and for being a 'neo-Evangelical' for speaking at the gatherings of the Church Congresses; they also denounced the appointment of 'a neo-Evangelical to the Protestant see of Liverpool'. Within the diocese there was widespread criticism of his failure to be more pro-active in promoting the building of the cathedral. Even today Ryle is not without his detractors, and his particular brand of evangelicalism is not appreciated even by some who call themselves Anglican Evangelicals. Yet while he is known and admired by many nonconformists, those outside evangelical circles have barely heard of him. However the republication of his books and tracts, particularly in the USA, bears witness to the continuing popularity of his work, and hopefully this book will encourage more people to discover his writings and to understand and appreciate the significance of Bishop J C Ryle, the prince of tract-writers.

TRAVEL INFORMATION

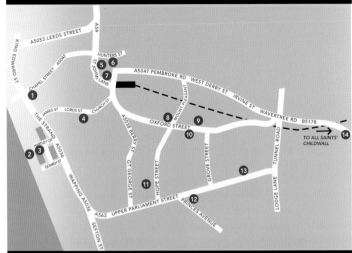

A MAP OF LIVERPOOL

KEY

1 ST NICHOLAS' CHURCH
2 TATE LIVERPOOL
3 MUSEUM
4 SITE OF ST PETER'S PRO-CATHEDRAL
5 MUSEUM
6 ART GALLERY

7 ST GEORGE'S HALL
8 R C CATHEDRAL
9 19 ABERCROMBY SQUARE
10 LIVERPOOL'S HEROES
11 ANGLICAN CATHEDRAL
12 ST MARGARET'S CHURCH

13 SITE OF ST NATHANIEL'S CHURCH
14 ALL SAINTS CHURCH CHILDWALL

TOURIST INFORMATION CENTRE

The 08 Place, Whitechapel, Liverpool L1 6DZ
www.visitliverpool.com/site/heritage/
search/08-place-p105371
☎ 0151 233 2008

Liverpool Cathedral (Anglican)

Liverpool Cathedral, St James' Mount,
Liverpool L1 7AZ
www.liverpoolcathedral.org.uk
☎ 0151 709 6271
Buses 80, 82 and 86

The foundation stone was laid in July
1904 and the rest of the building was

*Left: Liverpool's Anglican cathedral
was designed by the architect Giles
Gilbert Scott and the project became
his life's work. After winning the
original competition, he later
completely redesigned the building
and then continued to refine the design
until his death in 1960*

completed in stages: the Lady Chapel in 1910, the east end and eastern transepts in 1924, the central tower in 1942, the bridge and the first bay of the nave in 1961. The building was finally completed in October 1978. It is the largest Anglican cathedral ever built, and the tower is 331 feet (100 metres) high. Open daily 8.00am to 6.00pm.

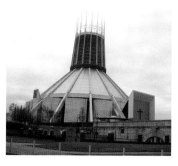

Above: *Liverpool's Roman Catholic cathedral was designed by the architect Frederick Gibberd, and erected between 1962 and 1967 and restored in the 1990s. The circular building is known as 'Paddy's Wigwam'*

Metropolitan Cathedral of Christ the King (Roman Catholic)

Cathedral House, Mount Pleasant, Liverpool L3 5TQ
www.liverpoolmetrocathedral.org.uk
© 0151 709 9222
Buses 80, 82 and 86

The foundation stone was laid on 5 June 1933, but the Second World War brought building work to a halt and by 1958 only the crypt (designed by Edwin Lutyens) had been completed. A competition was launched to design a new building and it was won by Frederick Gibberd. The new cathedral, which was erected in four stages, was consecrated on 14 May 1967. Open daily 8.00am to 6.00pm.

Abercromby Square 'Liverpool's Bloomsbury'

In 1880, no. 19 Abercromby Square became the Bishop's Palace, and from 1900 to 1915, no. 20 was the Bishop's Hostel for theological students. Today most of the Square is owned by the University of Liverpool.

Outside no. 19 is a blue plaque to Captain Noel Chavasse VC and Bar, MC, a son of Francis Chavasse, the second bishop of Liverpool. Noel was a medical doctor who died in Flanders in August 1917. He is commemorated in the impressive monument to 'Liverpool's heroes' outside no. 1, by a bust in the war memorial chapel of the Anglican cathedral, and by a UK postage stamp issued in September 2006. His identical twin brother Christopher, who also served in the First World War, was the Bishop of Rochester from 1940 to 1961.

All Saints' church, Childwall

Childwall Lane, Liverpool L16 0JW
www.allsaints-childwall.org
© 0151 737 2169
Buses 14, 79, 174 and 828

Childwall is about five miles east of Liverpool city centre and All Saints' church is off Childwall Valley Road. The building is the oldest mediaeval church in Liverpool, and over the centuries it has been enlarged and restored. From 1896 the incumbent was the retired missionary bishop, Peter Royston, who assisted the elderly Ryle in his episcopal duties. On her death in April 1889 Henrietta Ryle was interred in All Saints' churchyard, and on his death in June 1900 J C Ryle was interred in the adjacent grave.

To find the Ryle graves, turn left after leaving the south porch. Beyond the east end of the church the path then bears left and then divides. Turn left and then right and the two graves are located twenty-four rows down the slope on the left hand side.

A TIMELINE OF THE LIFE OF JOHN CHARLES RYLE

10 May 1816	Born at Park House, Macclesfield, Cheshire
February 1828	Entered Eton College, Windsor
15 May 1834	Matriculated Christ Church, Oxford
15 September 1836	Captain of the Macclesfield Troop (until 1841)
22 February 1838	Graduated BA (Oxford)
12 December 1841	Ordained deacon at Farnham Castle, Farnham, Surrey
12 December 1841	Curate of St Katharine, Exbury, Hampshire (until 1843)
11 December 1842	Ordained priest at Farnham Castle, Farnham, Surrey
1 November 1843	Rector of St Thomas, Winchester, Hampshire (until 1844)
14 February 1844	Rector of St Mary, Helmingham, Suffolk (until 1861)
29 October 1845	Married (1) Matilda Charlotte Louise Plumptre
18 June 1848	Death of Matilda Ryle. Interred at St Mary, Nonington, Kent
21 February 1850	Married (2) Jessie Elizabeth Walker
19 March 1859	Chaplain to the High Sheriff of Suffolk
19 May 1860	Death of Jessie Ryle. Interred at St Mary, Helmingham, Suffolk
11 September 1861	Vicar of All Saints, Stradbroke, Suffolk (until 1880)
24 October 1861	Married (3) Henrietta Amelia Clowes
15 May 1869	Appointed as the Rural Dean of Hoxne
8 June 1871	Graduated MA (Oxford)
3 February 1872	Appointed an honorary canon of Norwich cathedral
22 March 1880	Nominated as the Dean of Salisbury
4 May 1880	Awarded an honorary DD (Oxford)
11 June 1880	Consecrated as a bishop in York Minster
1 July 1880	Enthroned as the first Bishop of Liverpool (until 1900)
6 April 1889	Death of Henrietta Ryle. Interred at All Saints, Childwall, Liverpool
1 March 1900	Resigned as Bishop of Liverpool
10 June 1900	Died at Helmingham House, Lowestoft, Suffolk
14 June 1900	Interred at All Saints, Childwall, Liverpool

The forty-four churches consecrated during the episcopate of Bishop J C Ryle

8 September 1880	St Andrew, Maghull
10 September 1880	St John the Evangelist, Walton-on-the-Hill
30 November 1880	St Athanasius, Kirkdale
27 July 1881	St Cyprian, Edge Hill, Liverpool
1 August 1882	St Andrew, Wigan
17 October 1882	St Luke, Southport
1 November 1882	St Elizabeth of Hungary, Aspull
25 January 1883	St Stephen the Martyr, Edge Hill, Liverpool
6 December 1883	St Ambrose, Widnes
18 October 1884	St Gabriel, Toxteth Park, Liverpool
1 November 1884	All Saints, Princes Park, Liverpool
21 January 1885	St Agnes, Toxteth Park, Liverpool
18 March 1885	St John, Crossens
3 May 1885	St Chad, Everton
25 May 1886	St Mark, St Helens
27 May 1886	St Bede, Toxteth Park, Liverpool
21 June 1886	St Polycarp, Everton
17 November 1886	St Mary the Virgin, Waterloo
25 January 1887	St Paul, Widnes
2 August 1887	St Benedict, Everton
11 October 1887	St Philip, Southport
5 December 1887	St Mary, Ince-in-Makerfield
31 December 1887	St Peter, Woolton
8 May 1889	St Dunstan, Edge Hill, Liverpool
11 December 1889	St Leonard, Bootle
6 February 1890	St John the Evangelist, Everton
27 September 1890	St Anne, Stanley
2 December 1890	St Philip, Shiel Road, Liverpool
23 September 1891	St Peter, Warrington
5 December 1891	St Matthew, Bootle
25 June 1892	St John the Evangelist, Haydock
8 July 1892	Holy Trinity, Formby (and nave, chancel and transepts 12 May 1896)
17 June 1893	St Andrew, Toxteth Park, Liverpool
6 July 1893	St Thomas, Ashton-in-Makerfield
14 October 1893	All Saints, Sutton, St Helens
18 October 1893	St Luke, Warrington
1 November 1893	St Lawrence, Kirkdale
1 November 1894	St Gabriel, Huyton Quarry
25 February 1896	St Simon and St Jude, Anfield
5 June 1897	St Mark, Pemberton, Wigan
5 June 1897	St John the Baptist, New Springs
16 April 1898	Emmanuel, Southport
28 October 1899	St John the Evangelist, Hindley Green, Wigan (consecrated by Bishop Peter Royston)
2 December 1899	Christ Church, Waterloo (consecrated by Bishop Peter Royston)

BOOKS BY J C RYLE

Apart from the seven volumes of his *Expository Thoughts on the Gospels*, Ryle's key work was his eight volumes of collected tracts, *Home Truths*. Of these seventy-five tracts, two thirds reappeared in the trilogy of *Knots Untied*, *Old Paths*, *Practical Religion*, and in a fourth volume, *Holiness*, published to counter the perfectionist teaching of the day. Ryle was a moderate premillennialist, and his views on the second coming of Jesus appeared as *Coming Events and Present Duties*. Ryle published two volumes of historical biographies entitled *Christian Leaders of the Last Century* and *Facts and Men*. As a bishop, Ryle wrote fewer tracts, and his addresses and sermons were published as *Principles for Churchmen*, *The Upper Room* and *Charges and Addresses*. After his death some of Ryle's sermons preached over the previous sixty years were published as *The Christian Race*.

In all J C Ryle published about 200 tracts, some of which were later modified and given new titles before becoming chapters in his books. Today many of Ryle's books and tracts are still in print and are accessible on the Internet, and some of his books may be printed and bound to order.

	1	2	3
Expository Thoughts on the Gospels			
St Matthew (1856)	*		*
St Mark (1858)	*		
St Luke (1858)	*		
St John (1865, 1869, 1873)	*		
Home Truths (1851–1871)			
Hymns for the church on earth (1860)			
Coming events and present duties (1867, 1879)			*
The Christian leaders of the last century (1868)	*	*	
Shall we know one another? (1870)		*	
Church reform (1870)			
Knots untied (1874)		*	
Old paths (1877)	*		
Holiness (1877, 1879)		*	*
Practical religion (1878)	*		*
Boys and girls playing (1881)			*
Facts and men (1882) [Light from old times (1890)]		*	*
Principles for churchmen (1884)			
Disestablishment papers (1885)			
The upper room (1888)	*		
The Christian race and other sermons (1900)		*	*
Charges and addresses (1903)	*		

Publishers

1 Banner of Truth Trust **2** Charles Nolan (USA) **3** Evangelical Press

FURTHER READING

Peter Toon (editor) *J C Ryle. A Self Portrait* (Reiner Publications, USA, 1975)
Eric Russell, *That Man of Granite with the Heart of a Child* (Fearn, Ross-shire: Christian Focus, 2001)
Ian Farley, *J C Ryle. First Bishop of Liverpool* (Carlisle: Paternoster Press, 2000)
[Richard Hobson] *Richard Hobson of Liverpool* (Edinburgh: Banner of Truth Trust, 2003)
Oxford DNB [for articles on members of the Ryle family] (Oxford University Press, 2004)

ACKNOWLEDGEMENTS

I am thankful to the many archivists, librarians, local studies staff and local historians who have provided information and answered my many questions. I am indebted to those who have taken photographs—John Briggs, Roger Darsley, Judith Rodham, Dan Styles and particularly to Richard de Jong and Guy Munden. I am grateful too for the help given to me by Sebastian de Ferranti of Henbury Hall; Tim Brinton and Alan Hayward of Macclesfield; the Lord Tollemache of Helmingham Hall; Peter Haas of Helmingham; Mike Readman and David Streeter of Stradbroke, Val Jackson and John Vaughan of Liverpool; Geoffrey Ellis of Southport and Ray Collins of Lowestoft. I much appreciated the generous hospitality of Justin and Caroline Welby during my stay in Liverpool. I am thankful to Betty Hart for making available to me the miscellaneous notes of her husband, the late Geoffrey Hart. I have greatly valued making contact with members of the Plumptre family, and with two of the direct descendants of Bishop J C Ryle—John Ryle and his sister Caroline Walmsley. Finally, the series editor, Brian Edwards, has supported and encouraged the work throughout and has been very patient over the lengthy process of obtaining the photographs.

PICTURE ACKNOWLEDGEMENTS

Alan Bardsley 6, 10
Peter Beal 104
John Briggs 7, 14
Ray Collins 118
Roger Darsley 58
Richard de Jong 30–31, 33–34, 36, 39, 46–51, 110, 124
Brian Edwards 15, 38, 95, 98, 103
Geoffrey Ellis 105
Robert Gallagher 117
Debra Munden 59, 60, 61
Guy Munden 26–27, 87, 101, 105, 107, 110, 113
Mike Readman 68, 72–75, 78–79
Judith Rodham 44
Dan Styles 55–56, 77, 79–80, 85, 99–100
John Ryle 9

By kind permission of the following:

The estate of C. F. Tunnicliffe 6
The Lord Tollemache 54, 65
The Churches Conservation Trust 9–10
The Provost and Fellows of Eton College 15–17
Leamington Spa Art Gallery and Museum 42–43
London Metropolitan Archives 94, 106
The Dean and Chapter of Carlisle Cathedral *76*
The Dean and Chapter of Lincoln Cathedral 71
The Dean and Chapter of Liverpool Cathedral 114, 119
Macclesfield Silk Heritage Trust 10, 30
National Portrait Gallery, London 4, 25, 52, 57, 86, 90, 98, 110
The Norfolk Museums and Archaeological Service 58
The Professional Golfers' Association 62
Salford Local History Library 69

AUTHOR

Alan Munden is a Church of England minister who has served in churches in Cheltenham; Jesmond, Newcastle upon Tyne; Coventry and North Warwickshire. His main historical interest is in the development of Anglican Evangelicalism and, apart from his research and writing, he enjoys listening to classical music, walking and visiting tea shops. He lives in Newcastle upon Tyne and is married to Debra, a speech and language therapist, and they have two grown-up children, Caroline and Guy.

DAY ONE TRAVEL GUIDES

This series is unique: each book combines biography and history with travel guide. Notes, maps and photographs help you to explore Britain's distinctive heritage.

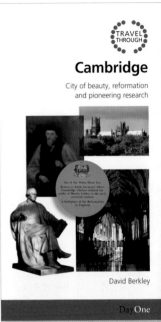

128 pages   **£10 EACH**

- PLACES OF INTEREST
- PACKED WITH COLOUR PHOTOS
- CLEAR ILLUSTRATED MAPS
- GREAT GIFT IDEA

OTHER TITLES IN THE SERIES

William Tyndale

John Calvin

John Knox

Martyrs of Mary Tudor

John Bunyan

William Grimshaw

William Carey

William Cowper

William Wilberforce

Murray McCheyne

CH Spurgeon

William Booth

Martyn Lloyd-Jones

CS Lewis

John Blanchard

Billy Graham

Frances Ridley Havergal

The British Museum with the Bible

Through Cambridge

Through Oxford

Through Israel

Through Egypt

Through Jordan

Through Rome

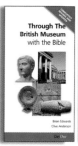
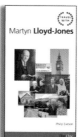
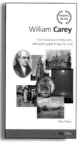

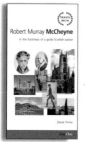

FOOTSTEPS OF THE PAST

A series of children's activity books twinned with the Travel Guides

ROMANS, GLADIATORS AND GAMES
In the British Museum, explore the Roman world of the first Christians

KINGS, PHARAOHS AND BANDITS
In the British Museum, explore the world of Abraham to Esther

WILLIAM TYNDALE
He was threatened, hunted, betrayed and killed so that we could have the Bible in English

JOHN BUNYAN
How a hooligan and soldier became a preacher, prisoner and famous writer

WILLIAM CAREY
The story of a country boy and shoe mender whose big dreams took him to India

WILLIAM BOOTH
The troublesome teenager who changed the lives of people no one else would touch

WILLIAM WILBERFORCE
The millionaire child who worked so hard to win the freedom of African slaves

C S LEWIS
The story of one of the world's most famous authors who sold over a hundred million books

The millionaire child who worked so hard to win the freedom of African slaves

William Wilberforce

ANDREW EDWARDS AND FLEUR THORNTON

Day One

Permission is given to copy the activity pages and associated text for use as class or group material